CYBER AUDITING UNLEASHED

ADVANCED SECURITY STRATEGIES FOR ETHICAL HACKERS

4 BOOKS IN 1

BOOK 1
MASTERING SECURITY AUDITING: ADVANCED TACTICS FOR ETHICAL HACKERS

BOOK 2
BEYOND THE BASICS: ADVANCED SECURITY AUDITING FOR ETHICAL HACKERS

BOOK 3
ETHICAL HACKING UNLEASHED: ADVANCED SECURITY AUDITING TECHNIQUES

BOOK 4
SECURITY AUDITING MASTERY: ADVANCED INSIGHTS FOR ETHICAL HACKERS

ROB BOTWRIGHT

Published by Rob Botwright
Library of Congress Cataloging-in-Publication Data
ISBN 978-1-83938-596-4
Cover design by Rizzo

Disclaimer

The contents of this book are based on extensive research and the best available historical sources. However, the author and publisher make no claims, promises, or guarantees about the accuracy, completeness, or adequacy of the information contained herein. The information in this book is provided on an "as is" basis, and the author and publisher disclaim any and all liability for any errors, omissions, or inaccuracies in the information or for any actions taken in reliance on such information.

The opinions and views expressed in this book are those of the author and do not necessarily reflect the official policy or position of any organization or individual mentioned in this book. Any reference to specific people, places, or events is intended only to provide historical context and is not intended to defame or malign any group, individual, or entity.

The information in this book is intended for educational and entertainment purposes only. It is not intended to be a substitute for professional advice or judgment. Readers are encouraged to conduct their own research and to seek professional advice where appropriate.

Every effort has been made to obtain necessary permissions and acknowledgments for all images and other copyrighted material used in this book. Any errors or omissions in this regard are unintentional, and the author and publisher will correct them in future editions.

BOOK 1 - MASTERING SECURITY AUDITING: ADVANCED TACTICS FOR ETHICAL HACKERS

BOOK 2 - BEYOND THE BASICS: ADVANCED SECURITY AUDITING FOR ETHICAL HACKERS

BOOK 3 - ETHICAL HACKING UNLEASHED: ADVANCED SECURITY AUDITING TECHNIQUES

BOOK 4 - SECURITY AUDITING MASTERY: ADVANCED INSIGHTS FOR ETHICAL HACKERS

Introduction

In an era defined by digital transformation and the relentless advancement of technology, cybersecurity has emerged as one of the most critical domains of our time. The rapid proliferation of connected devices and the ever-expanding digital landscape have given rise to unprecedented challenges and vulnerabilities, leaving organizations and individuals alike exposed to the relentless onslaught of cyber threats. In this digital battleground, the role of ethical hackers has become paramount.

Welcome to "Cyber Auditing Unleashed: Advanced Security Strategies for Ethical Hackers." This comprehensive book bundle is designed to be your ultimate guide in mastering the art of ethical hacking and advanced security auditing. Comprising four distinct volumes, each one dedicated to a specialized facet of the cybersecurity realm, this bundle equips you with the knowledge, skills, and insights needed to safeguard digital ecosystems and navigate the complex world of cyber threats.

Book 1 - Mastering Security Auditing: Advanced Tactics for Ethical Hackers: This volume serves as your initiation into the world of ethical hacking, offering a deep dive into the fundamental principles and practices that underpin the ethical hacker's role. From advanced vulnerability assessments to the art of penetration testing, you'll explore the critical components of cybersecurity and learn how to identify and mitigate potential risks.

Book 2 - Beyond the Basics: Advanced Security Auditing for Ethical Hackers: Building upon the foundation laid in the first book, this volume takes you on an exploration of advanced security auditing techniques. You'll delve into the complexities of cloud security, insider threat detection, and the intricacies of post-audit reporting and remediation. Here, you'll refine your expertise and prepare to face the evolving challenges of the digital landscape.

Book 3 - Ethical Hacking Unleashed: Advanced Security Auditing Techniques: This book ventures further into the world of ethical hacking, unveiling advanced techniques and tools essential for protecting digital assets. You'll gain proficiency in web application scanning, SQL injection, cross-site scripting (XSS) testing, wireless network enumeration, and cloud service models. Armed with this knowledge, you'll be well-prepared to combat sophisticated cyber threats.

Book 4 - Security Auditing Mastery: Advanced Insights for Ethical Hackers: In the final installment, you'll ascend to the pinnacle of cybersecurity mastery. This book provides advanced insights into insider threat indicators, behavioral analytics, user monitoring, documentation, reporting, and effective remediation strategies. You'll emerge from this volume as a seasoned cybersecurity professional, ready to tackle the most challenging security audits with confidence.

As you embark on this journey through the pages of "Cyber Auditing Unleashed," remember that ethical hacking is not merely a profession; it's a calling—a commitment to protecting the digital world from those who seek to exploit its vulnerabilities. The knowledge and skills you acquire within these books empower you to be a guardian of the digital realm, a sentinel of security, and a steward of ethical hacking principles.

So, let us begin this extraordinary odyssey into the world of cybersecurity, armed with the tools and insights needed to protect and defend the digital frontier. The challenges ahead are daunting, but with each page turned, you'll be better prepared to safeguard our increasingly interconnected world. Together, we embark on a mission to fortify the digital landscape and secure the future for generations to come.

BOOK 1
MASTERING SECURITY AUDITING
ADVANCED TACTICS FOR ETHICAL HACKERS

ROB BOTWRIGHT

Chapter 1: Understanding the Ethical Hacker's Role

Ethical hacking, also known as white-hat hacking, represents a critical and evolving field within the realm of cybersecurity.
It entails a deliberate and authorized attempt to probe, infiltrate, and assess an organization's information systems, networks, and applications, with the primary objective of identifying vulnerabilities and weaknesses.
Ethical hackers, often referred to as penetration testers or security auditors, employ a diverse set of tools, techniques, and methodologies to mimic the tactics of malicious hackers.
Their goal is to discover vulnerabilities before adversaries can exploit them, ultimately enhancing the overall security posture of the organization.
Ethical hacking plays a pivotal role in safeguarding sensitive data, mitigating security risks, and preventing cyberattacks that could lead to catastrophic consequences.
However, the ethical hacker's journey is not merely about technical expertise but also about adhering to a strict code of conduct and ethical principles.
The ethics of ethical hacking encompass integrity, transparency, and responsible disclosure.
Ethical hackers must conduct their activities with utmost honesty and integrity, ensuring that they have the necessary permissions and authorization from the target organization.
Transparency is essential, as ethical hackers need to provide clear documentation of their findings and the steps they took during the assessment.
Responsible disclosure implies that any vulnerabilities discovered should be reported promptly to the organization so that they can take appropriate actions to rectify them.

In essence, ethical hackers are not adversaries; they are allies in the relentless battle against cyber threats.

They operate within legal boundaries and uphold the law, distinguishing themselves from malicious hackers who engage in illegal activities.

To embark on the ethical hacker's journey, one must first acquire a strong foundation in computer science, networking, and cybersecurity fundamentals.

This knowledge forms the bedrock upon which the ethical hacker builds their skills and expertise.

Ethical hackers must also possess a profound understanding of the attacker's mindset, thinking like a hacker to anticipate and thwart potential threats.

Moreover, they should stay updated on emerging cybersecurity trends, threats, and vulnerabilities, as the threat landscape is constantly evolving.

In addition to technical skills, effective communication is a vital component of the ethical hacker's toolkit.

They must be adept at translating complex technical findings into understandable language for non-technical stakeholders.

This ability facilitates the reporting and remediation of identified vulnerabilities, ensuring that organizations can strengthen their defenses effectively.

The ethical hacker's journey involves continuous learning and professional growth.

Certifications, such as Certified Ethical Hacker (CEH) and Offensive Security Certified Professional (OSCP), validate their expertise and enhance their credibility in the field.

Yet, technical prowess alone is insufficient for ethical hacking; ethical hackers must also develop critical thinking and problem-solving skills.

They must approach each engagement with a methodical and systematic mindset, meticulously dissecting systems and applications to uncover hidden weaknesses.

During the reconnaissance phase, ethical hackers gather information about the target organization, understanding its infrastructure, technologies, and potential vulnerabilities.

This initial stage is crucial in crafting an effective attack strategy.

The next step involves vulnerability scanning, where ethical hackers use specialized tools to identify known vulnerabilities within the target environment.

These vulnerabilities may include outdated software, misconfigured systems, or weak password policies.

Once identified, the ethical hacker proceeds to exploit these vulnerabilities, attempting to gain unauthorized access or control over systems.

This phase simulates the actions of a malicious attacker, providing valuable insights into the organization's security posture.

Upon successful exploitation, ethical hackers aim to maintain access while minimizing detection.

They may escalate privileges, pivot through the network, or establish persistence to maintain control over compromised systems.

This phase requires not only technical skill but also discretion and subtlety to avoid triggering alarms or suspicion.

After thoroughly assessing the target environment, ethical hackers compile their findings into comprehensive reports.

These reports document identified vulnerabilities, their potential impact, and recommendations for remediation.

The ethical hacker must communicate these findings clearly and effectively to the organization's stakeholders.

Furthermore, they should assist in prioritizing and implementing security measures to address the identified weaknesses.

The ethical hacker's work doesn't end with the delivery of the report.

They may be called upon to support the organization during the remediation phase, providing guidance and expertise to ensure vulnerabilities are addressed effectively.

Additionally, ethical hackers play a crucial role in helping organizations establish proactive security practices.

They assist in the development of security policies, procedures, and guidelines that bolster the organization's resilience against future threats.

Ethical hacking is not a one-time endeavor; it's an ongoing commitment to protecting digital assets and sensitive information.

The ethical hacker's journey involves a perpetual cycle of assessment, reporting, and improvement.

It's a dynamic field that demands adaptability and a dedication to staying ahead of emerging threats.

In summary, the ethics of ethical hacking are rooted in principles of honesty, transparency, and responsible disclosure.

Ethical hackers are champions of cybersecurity, tirelessly working to safeguard organizations from the ever-present threat of cyberattacks.

Their journey is one of continuous learning, technical mastery, and unwavering commitment to securing the digital landscape.

As technology advances and cyber threats evolve, ethical hackers remain at the forefront of defense, ensuring that organizations can thrive in an increasingly digital world.

In the realm of ethical hacking, responsibilities and expectations are fundamental aspects that define the ethical hacker's role and impact on cybersecurity. Ethical hackers, often referred to as "white hats" or "security consultants," bear the crucial responsibility of safeguarding digital assets and sensitive information from malicious attackers. Their role is not only pivotal but also laden with ethical and moral considerations, setting them apart from black-hat hackers who engage in malicious activities. One of the primary responsibilities of an ethical hacker is to conduct authorized penetration tests and security assessments to identify vulnerabilities and weaknesses within an organization's information systems. To do so effectively, ethical hackers must adhere to a strict code of conduct and ethical guidelines, ensuring that their actions are legal, transparent, and well-documented. Transparency is a fundamental expectation in the ethical hacking domain, as ethical hackers are required to provide clear and comprehensive reports of their findings, methodologies, and actions taken during assessments. These reports serve as a critical bridge of communication between the ethical hacker and the organization, allowing for informed decisions and targeted remediation efforts. Furthermore, ethical hackers are expected to operate with the utmost integrity and honesty, maintaining a high level of professionalism and trustworthiness in their interactions with clients and stakeholders. Integrity extends to obtaining proper authorization and permissions before conducting any security assessment or penetration test, ensuring that all activities are within legal boundaries. Responsible disclosure is another key component of ethical hacking, emphasizing the ethical hacker's obligation to promptly report discovered vulnerabilities to the organization's security team. This proactive approach enables organizations to address vulnerabilities and security weaknesses before malicious actors can exploit them, ultimately enhancing overall cybersecurity. While conducting assessments, ethical hackers must adopt the mindset of an adversary, thinking critically and creatively to uncover potential attack vectors and vulnerabilities. This perspective allows ethical hackers to anticipate and counteract emerging threats effectively, staying one step ahead of malicious hackers. In addition to technical skills, effective communication is a vital skill for ethical hackers. They must be able to translate complex technical findings into language that non-technical stakeholders can understand, facilitating informed decision-making and remediation. Ethical hackers are also expected to provide guidance and recommendations for mitigating identified vulnerabilities and strengthening security measures. Their role extends beyond finding weaknesses; it includes helping organizations take proactive steps to improve their overall security posture. To be effective, ethical hackers should stay updated on emerging cybersecurity trends, vulnerabilities, and attack techniques. The dynamic nature of the cybersecurity landscape demands ongoing learning and adaptation to address evolving threats. Certifications, such as Certified Ethical Hacker (CEH) and Offensive Security Certified Professional (OSCP), validate the expertise and qualifications of ethical hackers, enhancing their credibility in the field. Technical prowess alone is not sufficient for ethical hacking; critical thinking and problem-solving skills are equally essential. Ethical hackers must approach each engagement with a systematic and methodical mindset, meticulously dissecting systems and applications to uncover hidden vulnerabilities. The journey of an ethical hacker often begins with the reconnaissance phase, where they gather information about the target organization, understanding its infrastructure, technologies, and potential weaknesses. This initial phase is crucial for crafting an effective strategy for the assessment. Following reconnaissance, ethical hackers move on to vulnerability scanning, using specialized tools to identify known vulnerabilities within the target environment. These vulnerabilities may include outdated software, misconfigured systems, or weak password policies. Once identified, the ethical hacker proceeds to exploit these vulnerabilities, attempting to gain unauthorized access or control over systems. This phase simulates the actions of a malicious attacker, providing valuable insights into the organization's security posture. Upon successful exploitation, ethical hackers aim to maintain access while minimizing detection. They may escalate privileges, pivot through the network, or establish persistence to maintain control over compromised systems. This phase requires not only technical skill but also discretion and subtlety to avoid triggering alarms or suspicion. After thoroughly assessing the target environment, ethical hackers compile their findings into comprehensive reports. These reports document identified vulnerabilities, their potential impact, and recommendations for remediation. The ethical hacker must communicate these findings clearly and effectively to the organization's stakeholders. Furthermore, they should assist in prioritizing and implementing security measures to address the identified weaknesses. The ethical hacker's work doesn't end with the delivery of the report. They may be called upon to support the organization during the remediation phase, providing guidance and expertise to ensure vulnerabilities are addressed effectively. Additionally, ethical hackers play a crucial role in helping organizations establish proactive security practices. They assist in the development of security policies, procedures, and guidelines that bolster the organization's resilience against future threats. Ethical hacking is not a one-time endeavor; it's an ongoing commitment to protecting digital assets and sensitive information. The ethical hacker's journey involves a perpetual cycle of assessment, reporting, and improvement. It's a dynamic field that demands adaptability and a dedication to staying ahead of emerging threats. In summary, the responsibilities and expectations of an ethical hacker encompass a broad spectrum of skills, ethics, and professionalism. Ethical hackers are not merely technical experts; they are guardians of cybersecurity, operating within legal boundaries to fortify defenses against ever-evolving threats. Their commitment to transparency, integrity, and responsible disclosure makes them indispensable allies in the ongoing battle against cyberattacks and data breaches. As technology advances and cyber threats evolve, ethical hackers remain at the forefront of defense, ensuring that organizations can thrive in an increasingly digital world.

Chapter 2: Navigating the Security Audit Landscape

Security audits are an essential component of maintaining a robust and resilient cybersecurity posture in today's digital landscape. They serve as a critical mechanism for assessing the effectiveness of an organization's security measures and identifying vulnerabilities. Security audits encompass various types, each tailored to specific aspects of an organization's infrastructure, operations, and compliance requirements. One of the most common types of security audits is the network security audit, which focuses on evaluating the security of an organization's network infrastructure. Network security audits involve the examination of firewalls, routers, switches, and other network devices to ensure they are configured correctly and protect against unauthorized access. This type of audit also assesses network segmentation, access controls, and intrusion detection systems. Another vital category of security audits is the application security audit, which concentrates on scrutinizing the security of software applications. Application security audits encompass both web and mobile applications, aiming to identify vulnerabilities such as SQL injection, cross-site scripting (XSS), and insecure authentication mechanisms. These audits are crucial to safeguarding sensitive data and preventing cyberattacks that target software vulnerabilities. Cloud security audits have gained prominence with the widespread adoption of cloud computing services. These audits assess the security of cloud-based infrastructures, including Infrastructure as a Service (IaaS), Platform as a Service (PaaS), and Software as a Service (SaaS) environments. Cloud security audits examine data encryption, identity and access management, and compliance with cloud-specific security standards. Furthermore, organizations often conduct physical security audits to evaluate the physical safeguards in place to protect their premises and assets. Physical security audits encompass access control systems, surveillance cameras, alarm systems, and perimeter security measures. They ensure that unauthorized individuals cannot gain physical access to critical facilities or equipment. One of the most critical types of security audits, particularly for organizations that handle sensitive data, is the compliance audit. These audits verify an organization's adherence to specific regulatory frameworks, industry standards, and legal requirements. For instance, healthcare organizations must comply with the Health Insurance Portability and Accountability Act (HIPAA), while financial institutions are subject to the Payment Card Industry Data Security Standard (PCI DSS). Conducting compliance audits helps organizations avoid legal penalties and reputational damage while ensuring the protection of sensitive data. In addition to these common types of security audits, organizations may also conduct wireless security audits. These audits assess the security of wireless networks, including Wi-Fi networks, Bluetooth connections, and mobile device management. They aim to identify vulnerabilities in wireless communications that could be exploited by attackers to gain unauthorized access. Furthermore, organizations may engage in social engineering audits, which test the human element of security. These audits involve simulated phishing attacks, phone-based impersonation, and other techniques to evaluate employee awareness and susceptibility to social engineering tactics. Another type of security audit gaining importance is the Internet of Things (IoT) security audit. As IoT devices proliferate, organizations must assess the security of these interconnected devices, ensuring they do not become entry points for cyberattacks. IoT security audits focus on device authentication, data encryption, and the overall security of IoT ecosystems. Moreover, some organizations may require specialized security audits, such as those related to industrial control systems (ICS) and supervisory control and data acquisition (SCADA) systems. These audits evaluate the security of critical infrastructure components, including power plants, water treatment facilities, and manufacturing plants. The goal is to protect these systems from cyber threats that could have catastrophic real-world consequences. The frequency of security audits varies depending on an organization's industry, regulatory requirements, and risk tolerance. Some organizations perform security audits annually or semi-annually, while others may conduct them more frequently to maintain a proactive security posture. The importance of security audits extends beyond vulnerability identification; they also play a crucial role in incident response and threat mitigation. When security incidents or breaches occur, audit logs and reports serve as valuable forensic evidence. They enable organizations to trace the source of an incident, identify the extent of the compromise, and implement measures to contain and eradicate threats. Moreover, security audits provide organizations with insights into areas where security investments should be prioritized. By identifying weaknesses and vulnerabilities, audits guide organizations in allocating resources to strengthen their defenses. In many cases, security audits are a requirement for obtaining cybersecurity insurance or demonstrating security compliance to customers and partners. Customers and partners often seek assurance that an organization's security measures are robust and effective. A comprehensive security audit can provide that assurance, bolstering trust and business relationships. Effective security audits involve a combination of automated tools and manual testing conducted by skilled security professionals. Automated tools assist in scanning networks, applications, and systems for known vulnerabilities and misconfigurations. However, human expertise is essential for identifying complex vulnerabilities, understanding context, and evaluating security controls comprehensively. Security auditors must possess a deep understanding of cybersecurity principles, attacker tactics, and the organization's specific environment and assets. Moreover, they should stay updated on emerging threats and evolving security standards to conduct thorough and relevant audits. The audit process typically begins with scoping, where the organization defines the objectives, boundaries, and areas to be audited. Scoping ensures that the audit focuses on critical assets and risks while avoiding unnecessary disruptions to operations. Following scoping, auditors conduct the actual assessment, which may involve a combination of vulnerability scanning, penetration testing, code review, and configuration analysis. Throughout the assessment, auditors collect data, analyze findings, and validate vulnerabilities. Communication is a crucial aspect of the audit process. Auditors must maintain open lines of communication with the organization's stakeholders, including IT teams, management, and compliance officers. This ensures that audit findings are well-understood, and remediation efforts can be coordinated effectively. Once the assessment is complete, auditors compile their findings into a detailed audit report. The report includes an executive summary, an overview of the assessment scope and methodology, a summary of findings, and recommendations for remediation. Each identified vulnerability or weakness should be documented with clear descriptions and severity ratings. Recommendations should specify actions to address the issues and enhance security controls. The audit report serves as a valuable resource for the organization to prioritize and implement security improvements. After receiving the report, the organization should promptly initiate remediation efforts to address the identified vulnerabilities. The effectiveness of these efforts should be verified through follow-up assessments or audits to ensure that security measures have been properly implemented and are effective in mitigating risks. In summary, security audits are a critical element of modern cybersecurity, encompassing various types tailored to specific aspects of an organization's security posture. They play a crucial role in identifying vulnerabilities, ensuring compliance with regulations, and enhancing overall security. Security audits are not a one-time endeavor but rather an ongoing commitment to maintaining a resilient cybersecurity posture in the face of evolving threats. Effective security audits require a combination of automated tools, skilled auditors, and open communication with stakeholders to provide organizations with actionable insights and recommendations for improvement.

Regulatory compliance auditing is a critical process that organizations undertake to ensure they adhere to specific laws, regulations, and industry standards relevant to their operations.
These audits are not only essential for legal reasons but also for maintaining trust with customers, partners, and stakeholders.
Regulatory requirements can vary widely depending on an organization's industry, location, and the nature of its activities.
Common examples of regulatory frameworks include the Health Insurance Portability and Accountability Act (HIPAA) for healthcare, the Payment Card Industry Data Security

Standard (PCI DSS) for payment card processing, and the General Data Protection Regulation (GDPR) for data privacy in the European Union.

The primary goal of regulatory compliance auditing is to assess an organization's adherence to these external requirements and identify areas where it may fall short.

These audits are often performed by internal audit teams, external auditors, or regulatory agencies themselves.

Auditors review policies, procedures, controls, and documentation to ensure that the organization's practices align with regulatory mandates.

Regulatory compliance audits typically involve a comprehensive examination of an organization's data handling practices, security measures, and privacy policies.

They may also assess the organization's internal processes for reporting, monitoring, and addressing compliance issues.

One key aspect of regulatory compliance auditing is the need for clear documentation.

Organizations must maintain thorough records of their compliance efforts, as well as any actions taken to rectify identified non-compliance.

Documentation serves as evidence of an organization's commitment to adhering to regulations and can be crucial in case of legal disputes or regulatory investigations.

The frequency of regulatory compliance audits can vary significantly.

Some regulations require annual audits, while others may necessitate more frequent assessments or audits triggered by specific events or changes in an organization's operations.

Regulatory compliance auditing is often intertwined with risk management.

By identifying and addressing compliance gaps, organizations can mitigate the risk of regulatory fines, legal liabilities, and reputational damage.

It also helps organizations avoid disruptions in their operations that could result from regulatory non-compliance.

During a regulatory compliance audit, auditors typically assess an organization's data security measures to ensure that they align with the specific requirements of the relevant regulations.

This may involve evaluating the encryption of sensitive data, access controls, authentication methods, and data retention policies.

In the case of healthcare organizations subject to HIPAA, for example, auditors would examine how patient data is handled, stored, and transmitted, ensuring that it complies with the regulation's strict privacy and security requirements.

Payment card processing entities subject to PCI DSS would be audited on their ability to protect cardholder data, including the use of secure networks, encryption, and regular vulnerability assessments.

In addition to data security, regulatory compliance audits often scrutinize an organization's privacy practices.

This includes how personal and sensitive information is collected, used, disclosed, and protected.

For example, organizations subject to GDPR must demonstrate that they have mechanisms in place to obtain consent for data processing, allow individuals to access and rectify their data, and report data breaches within specific timeframes.

Non-compliance with GDPR can result in severe financial penalties.

Furthermore, regulatory compliance audits evaluate an organization's documentation and reporting practices related to compliance.

Auditors assess whether policies and procedures are in place and that employees are adequately trained to follow them.

They also look for evidence that the organization conducts regular risk assessments and monitors compliance continuously.

Documentation should include records of risk assessments, incident reports, and any remediation efforts taken to address compliance issues.

Regulatory compliance audits extend beyond data security and privacy to encompass broader aspects of an organization's operations.

For instance, financial institutions subject to regulations like the Sarbanes-Oxley Act (SOX) must ensure that they have internal controls and reporting mechanisms in place to maintain financial transparency and prevent fraud.

These audits may involve a thorough examination of financial records, accounting practices, and governance processes.

In some cases, regulatory compliance audits may also involve assessing an organization's environmental practices and sustainability efforts.

Organizations operating in highly regulated industries, such as pharmaceuticals or energy, must demonstrate compliance with environmental regulations to avoid legal repercussions and reputational damage.

Compliance with environmental regulations often involves auditing practices related to waste disposal, emissions control, and adherence to sustainability standards.

Regulatory compliance audits are not solely about identifying non-compliance; they also provide organizations with an opportunity to improve their practices and enhance overall operational efficiency.

By addressing identified weaknesses and implementing recommended changes, organizations can streamline their processes, reduce risks, and build trust with stakeholders.

In summary, regulatory compliance auditing is a fundamental process for organizations across various industries.

It ensures that organizations adhere to specific laws, regulations, and industry standards relevant to their operations.

Compliance audits encompass data security, privacy, financial transparency, and other aspects of an organization's activities.

These audits are essential for mitigating risks, avoiding legal liabilities, and maintaining trust with customers, partners, and stakeholders.

Clear documentation and a commitment to addressing identified compliance gaps are crucial components of successful regulatory compliance audits.

Organizations that view compliance audits as an opportunity for improvement can not only achieve regulatory adherence but also enhance their overall operational efficiency and resilience.

Chapter 3: Advanced Vulnerability Assessment

Vulnerability scanning tools are instrumental in identifying weaknesses and vulnerabilities within an organization's network, systems, and applications. These tools play a pivotal role in proactive cybersecurity, helping organizations pinpoint potential entry points for malicious attackers before they can exploit them. Vulnerability scanning tools are designed to automate the process of assessing an organization's digital infrastructure for known vulnerabilities and misconfigurations. One of the primary advantages of these tools is their ability to perform comprehensive scans quickly and efficiently, saving time and resources. These scans involve the systematic examination of network devices, servers, operating systems, and software applications. They aim to uncover vulnerabilities that may be exploited by cybercriminals to gain unauthorized access or disrupt operations. The first step in using vulnerability scanning tools is configuring the scan parameters to align with the organization's objectives. Scans can be tailored to specific assets, target ranges, and compliance requirements, ensuring a focused and relevant assessment. Once the scan parameters are set, the tool initiates the scanning process, probing the target systems for known vulnerabilities and weaknesses. Vulnerability scanning tools rely on an extensive database of known vulnerabilities, which is continuously updated to keep pace with emerging threats. During a scan, the tool compares the configuration and software versions of scanned assets against this database, flagging any discrepancies or matches. When vulnerabilities are detected, the tool generates reports detailing the findings, including the severity of each vulnerability and potential impacts. These reports provide organizations with actionable insights into their security posture and help prioritize remediation efforts. Vulnerability scanning tools categorize vulnerabilities based on their severity, typically using a scale that ranges from low to critical. This severity rating helps organizations determine which vulnerabilities should be addressed immediately and which can be managed over time. In addition to severity ratings, vulnerability scanning reports often include detailed information about each identified vulnerability. This information may include a description of the vulnerability, its associated Common Vulnerability and Exposure (CVE) identifier, and recommended remediation steps. Some vulnerability scanning tools go a step further, providing links to official vendor patches or fixes that address the identified vulnerabilities. Organizations can use these reports to guide their remediation efforts, allowing them to address vulnerabilities effectively. Furthermore, vulnerability scanning tools offer flexibility in terms of scanning frequency. Organizations can choose to conduct scans on a regular basis, such as daily, weekly, or monthly, to continuously monitor their security posture. Regular scanning helps organizations detect new vulnerabilities that may emerge over time due to software updates, changes in configurations, or emerging threats. Additionally, vulnerability scanning tools offer different scanning modes to accommodate various organizational needs. For example, organizations can perform authenticated scans, which involve scanning assets with valid credentials to assess configurations accurately. Unauthenticated scans, on the other hand, simulate the actions of an external attacker by probing systems without access privileges. While authenticated scans offer more comprehensive insights, unauthenticated scans provide a broader view of potential vulnerabilities visible from the outside. Some advanced vulnerability scanning tools also offer penetration testing capabilities, allowing organizations to simulate real-world attacks and gauge their resilience. These tools combine vulnerability scanning with exploitation testing to assess an organization's ability to withstand attacks. Furthermore, vulnerability scanning tools often integrate with other cybersecurity solutions and workflows. Integration with security information and event management (SIEM) systems, for example, enables organizations to correlate vulnerability data with real-time threat information. This integration enhances an organization's ability to prioritize remediation efforts based on the current threat landscape. Moreover, vulnerability scanning tools often offer customization options, enabling organizations to create and tailor scanning policies to their specific needs. Customization may involve defining scan schedules, excluding certain assets from scans, or adjusting scanning parameters to align with industry standards and compliance requirements. Compliance is a significant driver for vulnerability scanning, as many regulations and standards mandate regular vulnerability assessments. For instance, the Payment Card Industry Data Security Standard (PCI DSS) requires organizations that handle payment card data to conduct regular vulnerability scans. Organizations in the healthcare sector must comply with the Health Insurance Portability and Accountability Act (HIPAA), which includes vulnerability scanning as a critical security measure. In summary, vulnerability scanning tools are indispensable in the realm of cybersecurity, providing organizations with a proactive means of identifying and addressing potential vulnerabilities and weaknesses. These tools automate the scanning process, saving time and resources, and generate detailed reports that guide remediation efforts. Regular scanning and customization options enable organizations to adapt vulnerability assessments to their specific needs and compliance requirements. Moreover, vulnerability scanning tools often integrate with other security solutions, enhancing an organization's ability to correlate vulnerability data with real-time threat information. As the cybersecurity landscape evolves, vulnerability scanning remains a fundamental practice to safeguard digital assets and maintain a resilient security posture.

Risk assessment and prioritization are essential processes in the realm of cybersecurity, enabling organizations to systematically evaluate and address potential threats to their digital assets and operations.

These processes play a pivotal role in proactively managing and mitigating risks, reducing the likelihood of security incidents, and minimizing their potential impact.

At its core, risk assessment involves the identification, evaluation, and analysis of vulnerabilities, threats, and potential security incidents that could affect an organization.

The goal is to gain a comprehensive understanding of the organization's risk landscape and the factors that contribute to security vulnerabilities.

One of the fundamental elements of risk assessment is vulnerability identification, which entails identifying weaknesses, flaws, or gaps in an organization's digital infrastructure, systems, or processes that could be exploited by malicious actors.

These vulnerabilities can range from unpatched software and misconfigured systems to insecure authentication mechanisms and weak password policies.

Threat identification is another critical aspect of risk assessment, focusing on recognizing potential sources of harm or danger that could exploit identified vulnerabilities.

Threats may include external attackers, insiders with malicious intent, natural disasters, or technological failures.

The process of risk assessment typically involves evaluating the potential impact of identified threats and vulnerabilities, as well as their likelihood of occurrence.

This assessment allows organizations to prioritize risks based on their severity and probability, ensuring that resources are allocated efficiently to address the most critical issues.

Risk assessment methodologies often use qualitative and quantitative approaches to assign values and rankings to risks, aiding in prioritization efforts.

Qualitative methods involve expert judgment and subjective analysis, while quantitative methods use data-driven calculations and measurements to assess risks.

Once risks have been identified, evaluated, and ranked, organizations can develop risk mitigation strategies and action plans.

These strategies may include implementing security controls, policies, and procedures to reduce the likelihood of risk occurrence or limit its impact.

Security controls can encompass a wide range of measures, including access controls, encryption, intrusion detection systems, and employee training programs.

Additionally, organizations must consider the potential cost of implementing risk mitigation measures versus the potential cost of a security incident, helping to make informed decisions.

Prioritization is a critical step in the risk assessment process, as it guides organizations in determining which risks should be addressed first and with what level of urgency.

Risk prioritization takes into account various factors, such as the potential harm to the organization, the likelihood of risk occurrence, the organization's risk tolerance, and the available resources for mitigation.

Some organizations use risk matrices or risk heat maps to visualize and prioritize risks, providing a clear and intuitive way to make decisions.

High-priority risks, often referred to as critical risks, are those with the potential for significant harm to the organization and a high likelihood of occurrence.

These risks typically require immediate attention and allocation of resources to implement mitigation measures.

Medium-priority risks, while not as severe as critical risks, still pose a noteworthy threat to the organization and should be addressed in a timely manner.

Low-priority risks are those with a lower potential impact or a lower likelihood of occurrence, making them less urgent for mitigation.

However, it is essential to monitor and reassess these risks regularly, as the risk landscape can change over time.

Risk assessment and prioritization are iterative processes, requiring continuous monitoring and adjustment.

As the organization's technology landscape evolves, new vulnerabilities and threats may emerge, necessitating ongoing assessments to stay proactive.

Furthermore, external factors, such as changes in regulations or the threat landscape, can influence the organization's risk profile, requiring adjustments to risk mitigation strategies.

Communication and collaboration are integral components of effective risk assessment and prioritization.

Organizations should foster an environment where stakeholders from various departments, including IT, security, legal, and compliance, can collaborate to assess and prioritize risks collectively.

This interdisciplinary approach ensures that all perspectives are considered, resulting in more robust risk assessments and better-informed prioritization decisions.

In some cases, organizations may also engage third-party experts or consultants to provide an objective assessment of risks and help prioritize mitigation efforts.

Risk assessment and prioritization are not isolated processes; they are integral to an organization's overall risk management strategy.

They feed into the development of a risk management plan, which outlines how the organization intends to address identified risks over time.

This plan should include specific actions, timelines, responsible parties, and success criteria for each risk mitigation effort.

Regular reporting and communication of risk assessment findings and prioritization decisions are crucial for maintaining transparency and accountability within the organization.

Furthermore, organizations must regularly review and update their risk assessment methodologies and criteria to ensure that they remain relevant and effective.

In summary, risk assessment and prioritization are fundamental processes in cybersecurity, enabling organizations to identify, evaluate, and address potential threats and vulnerabilities systematically.

These processes guide organizations in making informed decisions about how to allocate resources to mitigate risks effectively.

Risk assessment involves identifying vulnerabilities and threats, evaluating their potential impact and likelihood, and ranking risks based on their severity.

Effective prioritization ensures that high-priority risks are addressed promptly, reducing the organization's exposure to security incidents.

Risk assessment and prioritization are ongoing and iterative processes that require collaboration, communication, and adaptation to changes in the risk landscape and organizational priorities.

By integrating risk assessment and prioritization into their overall risk management strategy, organizations can build resilience against emerging threats and maintain a strong security posture.

Chapter 4: Penetration Testing Fundamentals

Planning and scoping penetration tests are critical initial steps in conducting successful security assessments that simulate real-world attacks on an organization's systems, networks, and applications.

The planning and scoping phase lays the foundation for the entire penetration testing process, influencing the depth, breadth, and effectiveness of the assessment.

To begin, it's essential to define the objectives and goals of the penetration test, as this shapes the testing scope and helps align the assessment with the organization's specific security needs.

These objectives could include identifying vulnerabilities, assessing the security posture of a specific system or application, or evaluating the effectiveness of existing security controls.

In addition to objectives, it's crucial to determine the scope of the penetration test, which defines what systems, assets, and environments will be included in the assessment.

Scope considerations should encompass factors such as the target infrastructure, the number of systems to be tested, and the types of vulnerabilities that will be evaluated.

The scope should also clarify any limitations or constraints, such as blackout periods when testing should not occur or systems that must not be disrupted during the assessment.

Scoping also involves defining the rules of engagement, which outline the boundaries and rules that penetration testers must follow during the assessment.

Rules of engagement typically specify which systems are fair game for testing, the hours during which testing is allowed, and the extent to which testers can exploit vulnerabilities.

Moreover, scoping should consider the level of access granted to testers, including whether they have full access to systems or are limited to external assessments without internal network access.

A critical aspect of scoping is identifying the testing methodology and approach that aligns with the organization's objectives and risk tolerance.

The methodology determines how the penetration test will be conducted, whether it follows a black-box, white-box, or gray-box approach.

In a black-box test, testers have no prior knowledge of the target environment, simulating the perspective of an external attacker.

In contrast, a white-box test provides testers with complete knowledge of the target systems, simulating an insider's perspective.

A gray-box test falls somewhere in between, offering limited knowledge of the environment.

The scoping phase also involves identifying the testing team, including the penetration testers and their roles in the assessment.

Selecting qualified and certified penetration testers is essential to ensure the assessment's effectiveness and reliability.

Furthermore, organizations should establish communication channels between the testing team and the internal stakeholders, such as IT and security teams, to facilitate coordination and information sharing.

Once the scope is well-defined, organizations should create a detailed project plan outlining the testing timeline, milestones, and deliverables.

This plan helps keep the assessment on track, ensuring that objectives are met within the allocated time frame.

To ensure a smooth and efficient testing process, organizations must obtain proper authorization and consent from stakeholders, including legal and compliance teams.

Unauthorized penetration testing can lead to legal and regulatory consequences, so obtaining clear authorization is paramount.

Furthermore, organizations should consider the potential impact of the assessment on their production systems and services.

It's essential to coordinate with relevant teams to minimize disruptions during testing and have a plan in place for responding to unexpected incidents or outages.

Risk management is another integral aspect of the planning and scoping phase.

Organizations should assess the risks associated with the penetration test and develop contingency plans to address potential issues.

For instance, if an unexpected vulnerability is discovered during testing that could lead to a system compromise, there should be a plan in place for immediate mitigation.

Clear communication and reporting procedures should also be established to ensure that any identified vulnerabilities are reported promptly and accurately to the organization's stakeholders.

The scoping phase should also account for post-test activities, such as debriefing sessions with the testing team to discuss findings and recommendations.

These sessions provide an opportunity to clarify any questions, validate findings, and ensure that all parties have a clear understanding of the assessment results.

Additionally, organizations should develop a comprehensive report that includes the assessment's objectives, scope, methodology, findings, recommendations, and an executive summary.

This report serves as a valuable resource for stakeholders to understand the assessment's outcomes and take appropriate actions.

In summary, the planning and scoping of penetration tests are critical components of a successful security assessment.

Defining clear objectives, scope, rules of engagement, and methodology sets the foundation for an effective assessment that aligns with an organization's specific security needs.

Effective scoping involves selecting a qualified testing team, obtaining proper authorization, and establishing communication and risk management procedures.

By meticulously planning and scoping penetration tests, organizations can identify vulnerabilities, assess their security posture, and take proactive steps to enhance their cybersecurity defenses.

Information gathering techniques are essential processes in cybersecurity and ethical hacking, serving as the initial phase of any security assessment or penetration testing endeavor.

These techniques involve the systematic collection of data, intelligence, and insights about an organization's digital assets, infrastructure, and online presence.

The primary objective of information gathering is to gather a comprehensive understanding of the target environment, identifying potential vulnerabilities and attack vectors that can be exploited by malicious actors.

One of the foundational methods employed in information gathering is passive reconnaissance, which entails gathering information without directly interacting with the target.

Passive reconnaissance often begins with open-source intelligence (OSINT) collection, which involves gathering publicly available information from sources such as websites, social media, and publicly accessible databases.

OSINT provides valuable insights into an organization's employees, technologies, partners, and online footprint.

Another passive reconnaissance technique involves DNS enumeration, which aims to discover subdomains, mail servers, and other network-related information by querying DNS servers.

This technique can reveal valuable details about an organization's network infrastructure and technology stack.

Moreover, passive reconnaissance often involves WHOIS queries to retrieve information about domain registrants, administrators, and contact details, shedding light on the organization's web presence.

Another essential aspect of information gathering is active reconnaissance, which involves direct interaction with the target to gather data and intelligence.

Active reconnaissance techniques are more intrusive and may be less stealthy than passive methods, as they entail sending requests and probes to target systems.

One common active reconnaissance technique is port scanning, where tools like Nmap are used to identify open ports and services running on target systems.

Port scanning helps determine the attack surface and potential entry points into the target's network.

Additionally, banner grabbing involves connecting to open ports and collecting banners and service information to identify specific software versions and configurations.

Service enumeration further refines the information gathered from banner grabbing by identifying running services and associated vulnerabilities.

Network scanning techniques, such as ARP scanning and ICMP probing, can reveal information about hosts within a local network, helping assess internal security.

Moreover, vulnerability scanning tools like Nessus or OpenVAS are often employed during the information gathering phase to identify known vulnerabilities in target systems.

These tools automate the process of scanning and identifying vulnerabilities in networked devices and applications.

Social engineering, although not solely a technical technique, is a crucial component of information gathering.

Social engineering involves manipulating individuals or employees within the target organization to reveal sensitive information or grant unauthorized access.

Phishing, pretexting, and baiting are common social engineering tactics used to extract valuable information.

Additionally, dumpster diving and physical reconnaissance can be used to gather information from discarded documents or to assess the physical security of an organization.

While technical methods are essential, it's crucial not to underestimate the human factor in information gathering.

Once data has been collected, the next step is to organize and analyze it systematically.

Data organization involves categorizing and structuring information for effective analysis.

This may involve creating databases, spreadsheets, or documentation that organizes the data into manageable and meaningful segments.

Data analysis is a critical phase in information gathering, as it transforms raw data into actionable intelligence.

Analyzing data involves identifying patterns, relationships, and insights that can inform the assessment's objectives.

Organizations often employ data analysis tools and techniques to mine large datasets for valuable information.

For instance, data correlation and visualization tools can help identify connections between disparate pieces of information.

Furthermore, data analysis can uncover potential attack vectors, weaknesses, and vulnerabilities within the target environment.

It can also help assess the organization's security posture, identifying areas where security controls may be lacking or ineffective.

Effective information gathering also involves verifying the accuracy and reliability of collected data.

False or outdated information can lead to incorrect assumptions and misguided decisions during a security assessment.

Verification techniques may include cross-referencing information from multiple sources, conducting additional reconnaissance to validate findings, or utilizing trusted intelligence feeds.

It's essential to ensure that the information gathered is up-to-date and relevant to the assessment's objectives.

Information gathering is an ongoing process, as the security landscape and the target environment evolve over time.

Regular assessments and continuous monitoring of the target are essential to maintain an accurate understanding of potential risks and vulnerabilities.

In summary, information gathering techniques are the foundation of effective cybersecurity assessments and ethical hacking endeavors.

These techniques involve passive and active reconnaissance methods to collect data and intelligence about the target environment.

Data organization and analysis are crucial steps in transforming raw data into actionable insights that inform the assessment's objectives.

Verification of gathered information is essential to ensure its accuracy and reliability.

By employing systematic and well-structured information gathering techniques, organizations can enhance their security posture, identify potential vulnerabilities, and proactively defend against cyber threats.

Chapter 5: Network Security Analysis

A network architecture review is a comprehensive examination of an organization's network infrastructure, aiming to assess its design, configuration, and overall effectiveness.

This critical process provides organizations with valuable insights into the current state of their network and identifies areas for improvement.

The network architecture review begins by examining the organization's network topology, which defines how devices and components are interconnected.

This includes an assessment of the network's physical layout, such as the placement of routers, switches, and access points, as well as its logical structure, which determines how data flows between network segments.

The review also evaluates the network's scalability, considering its ability to accommodate growth and increasing demands for bandwidth and resources.

A fundamental aspect of the review is assessing the network's security posture.

This involves examining security measures such as firewalls, intrusion detection and prevention systems, and access control policies to determine their effectiveness in safeguarding the network from external threats.

Additionally, the review considers the organization's compliance with security best practices and relevant regulations.

Network segmentation is another critical area of focus in a network architecture review.

This involves dividing the network into smaller, isolated segments to enhance security and control network traffic.

The review evaluates the segmentation strategy, ensuring that it aligns with the organization's security requirements and access control policies.

Furthermore, the review assesses the network's redundancy and failover mechanisms to ensure high availability and resilience.

Redundancy involves duplicating critical network components to mitigate the risk of network downtime, while failover mechanisms automatically switch to backup components in case of a failure.

Network performance is a key consideration in the review, encompassing factors such as latency, throughput, and packet loss.

Performance testing and analysis help identify bottlenecks, congestion points, or other issues that may impact the network's efficiency and user experience.

The network architecture review delves into the organization's routing and switching configuration, evaluating the routing protocols in use and the efficiency of the routing tables.

It also examines the switching infrastructure to ensure that it provides optimal data forwarding and VLAN management.

Wireless network architecture is assessed as well, examining the placement and configuration of wireless access points, as well as security measures like WPA3 encryption and network segmentation for guest and internal users.

The review also considers the organization's use of virtual private networks (VPNs) to secure remote access and data transmission over public networks.

A crucial component of the network architecture review is the assessment of network monitoring and management tools.

This includes evaluating the organization's use of network monitoring solutions to detect anomalies, performance issues, and security threats in real-time.

Effective network management tools help streamline network administration and troubleshooting.

In addition, the review considers the organization's policies and procedures related to network administration, including user access management, password policies, and incident response plans.

Documentation and asset management are important aspects of the review, ensuring that an up-to-date inventory of network devices and configurations is maintained.

This documentation is essential for troubleshooting, auditing, and compliance purposes.

The network architecture review also explores the organization's disaster recovery and business continuity strategies, assessing their ability to minimize network downtime in the event of a catastrophic event.

It considers factors such as data backup and recovery processes, off-site data storage, and backup power systems.

Furthermore, the review evaluates the organization's use of cloud services and their integration into the network architecture.

This includes assessing the security of cloud connections, data encryption, and the management of cloud resources.

Finally, the network architecture review examines the organization's future network plans and technology roadmap.

This involves considering emerging technologies such as software-defined networking (SDN), network virtualization, and the implementation of IPv6.

The goal is to ensure that the organization's network architecture can evolve to meet changing business needs and technological advancements.

In summary, a network architecture review is a comprehensive evaluation of an organization's network infrastructure, covering aspects such as design, security, performance, and management.

It provides organizations with insights into the current state of their network and helps identify areas for improvement to enhance security, efficiency, and scalability.

By conducting regular network architecture reviews, organizations can adapt to evolving technology trends, strengthen their network defenses, and ensure the reliability of their network infrastructure.

Traffic analysis and anomaly detection are fundamental components of network security, offering organizations the ability to monitor, identify, and respond to abnormal network behavior.

These techniques play a crucial role in safeguarding against various cyber threats and ensuring the integrity and availability of network resources.

Traffic analysis involves the examination of network traffic patterns and data flows to gain insights into normal network behavior.

It provides a baseline of what is considered typical for an organization's network, which can then be used to identify deviations or anomalies.

One of the primary goals of traffic analysis is to detect and respond to unauthorized or malicious activities, such as network intrusions, data exfiltration, or denial-of-service attacks.

To achieve this, organizations employ a range of network monitoring tools and techniques.

Network traffic can be categorized into different types, including inbound and outbound traffic, internal and external traffic, and user-generated versus system-generated traffic.

Understanding these distinctions is essential for effective traffic analysis.

Intrusion detection systems (IDS) and intrusion prevention systems (IPS) are commonly used tools for traffic analysis and anomaly detection.

These systems inspect network traffic for suspicious patterns or signatures that may indicate a security breach.

IDS systems raise alerts or notifications when anomalies are detected, while IPS systems can take automated actions to block or mitigate threats.

Network flow analysis is another traffic analysis technique that involves examining network flows or connections between devices and services.

Flow analysis provides information about the source and destination of traffic, the volume of data exchanged, and the duration of connections.

This data can be used to detect anomalies, such as unusual traffic patterns or connections to known malicious IP addresses.

Furthermore, deep packet inspection (DPI) techniques allow for the examination of the actual content within network packets.

DPI can reveal specific application-level behaviors and identify potentially malicious payloads or data exfiltration attempts.

Anomaly detection is a complementary approach to traffic analysis, focusing on the identification of unusual or unexpected network behavior.

Anomalies can manifest in various forms, such as sudden traffic spikes, unusual port activity, or deviations from established network patterns.

Machine learning and artificial intelligence (AI) algorithms are often employed in anomaly detection systems to analyze large volumes of network data and identify deviations.

Behavioral analysis, a subset of anomaly detection, focuses on understanding typical user and system behavior on the network.

By establishing baseline behavior for users and devices, anomalies, such as unauthorized access or abnormal data transfer, can be more readily identified.

Heuristic anomaly detection relies on predefined rules and thresholds to detect anomalies.

For example, it may trigger an alert when an unusually large number of login attempts occur within a short time frame.

Signature-based detection is a technique that compares network traffic against known attack signatures or patterns.

When a match is found, it signifies a potential threat or anomaly.

Intrusion detection and prevention systems often incorporate signature-based detection methods.

Statistical anomaly detection, on the other hand, utilizes statistical models to identify deviations from expected network behavior.

This method can be highly effective in identifying subtle anomalies that may not trigger traditional rule-based or signature-based detection.

Flow-based anomaly detection assesses network flows and connections, identifying unusual flow characteristics, such as unusual traffic volume or duration.

It is particularly useful for identifying distributed denial-of-service (DDoS) attacks and network scanning activities.

Real-time anomaly detection is a critical aspect of network security, as it enables organizations to respond swiftly to emerging threats.

When anomalies are detected, alerts or notifications are generated, allowing security teams to investigate and take appropriate actions.

These actions may include isolating affected devices, blocking malicious traffic, or implementing additional security measures.

Continuous monitoring and analysis are essential for staying ahead of evolving threats, as new attack techniques and vulnerabilities emerge regularly.

Additionally, organizations can enhance their anomaly detection capabilities by integrating threat intelligence feeds and collaborating with external security partners to gain insights into emerging threats.

In summary, traffic analysis and anomaly detection are vital components of modern network security strategies.

They enable organizations to monitor network traffic, identify deviations from normal behavior, and respond swiftly to potential threats.

By employing a combination of traffic analysis and anomaly detection techniques, organizations can bolster their cybersecurity defenses and protect against a wide range of cyber threats.

Chapter 6: Web Application Auditing

Web application scanning tools are indispensable assets in the arsenal of modern cybersecurity professionals, providing the means to assess the security posture of web applications and identify vulnerabilities that could be exploited by malicious actors.

These tools play a critical role in ensuring the confidentiality, integrity, and availability of web-based systems and the sensitive data they handle.

Web applications have become ubiquitous in today's digital landscape, serving as the backbone of online services, e-commerce platforms, and business-critical systems.

However, their widespread use also makes them attractive targets for cyberattacks, necessitating proactive security measures, including regular scanning and assessment.

Web application scanning tools, often referred to as web vulnerability scanners or web application security scanners, automate the process of identifying vulnerabilities in web applications.

They simulate real-world attacks, probing web applications for common security issues, such as injection attacks, cross-site scripting (XSS), cross-site request forgery (CSRF), and insecure authentication mechanisms.

One of the primary advantages of web application scanning tools is their efficiency in scanning large and complex web applications, which may consist of numerous pages, forms, and functionalities.

Manual security assessments of such applications can be time-consuming and error-prone, making automation an essential aspect of modern cybersecurity practices.

Web application scanning tools typically operate in one of two modes: black-box or white-box.

In a black-box approach, the scanner has no prior knowledge of the web application's internal architecture or code.

It behaves like an external attacker, interacting with the application as an end user would, sending requests and analyzing responses to identify vulnerabilities.

Conversely, in a white-box approach, the scanner has access to the application's source code or detailed documentation, allowing for a more in-depth analysis of potential vulnerabilities.

White-box scanning can uncover vulnerabilities that may not be apparent through black-box testing alone.

Some web application scanning tools also offer a gray-box approach, which combines elements of both black-box and white-box testing.

Web application scanning tools follow a systematic process that typically includes the following steps:

URL Discovery: The scanner starts by identifying the web application's URLs and endpoints, systematically crawling the site's pages and forms.

Vulnerability Detection: The tool actively probes the application for known vulnerabilities, such as SQL injection, XSS, and CSRF.

Authentication Testing: If the application requires user authentication, the scanner attempts to authenticate and assess the security of the authentication mechanism.

Session Management Analysis: The tool examines how the application manages user sessions, looking for vulnerabilities that could lead to unauthorized access.

Data Input Validation: Scanners test how the application handles user input, checking for security flaws that could enable attackers to manipulate data.

Output Encoding Analysis: The tool assesses how the application encodes output to prevent XSS attacks and other forms of data injection.

Reporting: Once the scan is complete, the tool generates a comprehensive report that outlines discovered vulnerabilities, their severity, and recommendations for remediation.

Web application scanning tools offer a wide range of features and capabilities to accommodate different use cases and security requirements.

Some tools focus on simplicity and ease of use, making them suitable for small businesses and organizations with limited cybersecurity expertise.

Others provide advanced features and customization options for experienced security professionals and large enterprises.

Common features of web application scanning tools include the ability to scan multiple web applications simultaneously, integration with continuous integration/continuous deployment (CI/CD) pipelines, and support for scanning APIs and mobile applications.

Scanners may also offer features for scanning web services and identifying vulnerabilities in underlying server components, such as the web server, application server, and database.

Moreover, some web application scanning tools incorporate machine learning and artificial intelligence (AI) techniques to enhance their ability to detect and prioritize vulnerabilities accurately.

These technologies can help reduce false positives and provide more precise results, enabling organizations to focus their resources on addressing genuine security risks.

While web application scanning tools are invaluable assets for identifying vulnerabilities, they are not a panacea for web application security.

Security professionals must follow best practices, such as secure coding, input validation, and patch management, to ensure the ongoing security of web applications.

Additionally, organizations should conduct regular security assessments, including manual penetration testing, to complement automated scanning efforts.

Furthermore, vulnerability scanning is only one component of a comprehensive web application security program.

Organizations must also implement robust access controls, monitoring, and incident response procedures to protect against evolving threats.

In summary, web application scanning tools are indispensable tools in the fight against web-based vulnerabilities and cyber threats.

They automate the process of identifying security issues in web applications, helping organizations maintain the security and integrity of their online assets.

However, they should be used in conjunction with other security measures and best practices to ensure comprehensive web application security.

SQL injection and cross-site scripting (XSS) are two of the most prevalent and potentially devastating web application vulnerabilities, and robust testing methods are essential to identify and mitigate these threats effectively.

SQL injection occurs when malicious SQL queries are injected into input fields or parameters of a web application, enabling attackers to manipulate the application's database.

This vulnerability arises from improper handling of user input, allowing attackers to execute unauthorized database operations and access sensitive information.

To test for SQL injection vulnerabilities, security professionals typically use various techniques to inject SQL code into input fields and assess the application's response.

This testing can include inputs like single quotes, double quotes, SQL keywords, and payloads designed to retrieve data from the database.

Testers analyze the application's responses, looking for error messages, data leaks, or other signs of successful SQL injection.

It is crucial to conduct both manual and automated testing to comprehensively evaluate an application's susceptibility to SQL injection.

Automated tools can quickly identify common SQL injection vulnerabilities, while manual testing allows testers to explore the application's behavior in more detail and uncover subtle issues.

Cross-site scripting (XSS) is another widespread vulnerability that occurs when an application improperly handles user-generated content and allows malicious scripts to be executed within the context of a user's browser.

XSS vulnerabilities can have severe consequences, such as stealing user credentials, session hijacking, or defacement of web pages.

Testing for XSS vulnerabilities involves injecting malicious scripts into input fields or parameters and observing how the application processes and renders the injected content.

Testers use payloads like script tags, event handlers, and encoded scripts to verify if the application reflects the injected code back to users.

They assess the application's security controls, such as input validation and output encoding, to determine if they effectively mitigate XSS risks.

XSS testing includes various types, such as stored XSS, reflected XSS, and DOM-based XSS, each requiring different testing approaches.

Like SQL injection testing, a combination of automated scanning tools and manual testing is recommended for comprehensive XSS assessment.

Automated tools can quickly identify common XSS vulnerabilities, while manual testing allows testers to explore different attack vectors and assess the impact of vulnerabilities.

In both SQL injection and XSS testing, testers should follow ethical hacking practices and obtain proper authorization before testing web applications.

Unauthorized testing can disrupt services, compromise data, and lead to legal consequences.

Testing should be conducted in controlled environments or against applications specifically designed for security assessment.

Testers must also prioritize the responsible disclosure of any vulnerabilities they discover, allowing organizations to remediate issues before they can be exploited maliciously.

Regular testing for SQL injection and XSS vulnerabilities is essential for maintaining the security of web applications.

Vulnerabilities can emerge as applications evolve, and new attack vectors may be discovered over time.

To stay ahead of potential threats, organizations should integrate security testing into their development and deployment processes, including continuous integration and continuous deployment (CI/CD) pipelines.

Furthermore, security training and awareness programs should be implemented to educate developers and testers about best practices for preventing and mitigating SQL injection and XSS vulnerabilities.

Preventing SQL injection and XSS vulnerabilities requires a proactive approach, including input validation, parameterized queries, and output encoding.

Input validation involves examining and validating user input to ensure it adheres to expected formats and values.

For example, if an application expects a numerical input, it should validate that the input consists only of digits and does not contain malicious characters.

Parameterized queries, also known as prepared statements, are database query templates that separate user input from SQL code.

They prevent attackers from injecting malicious SQL code by treating user input as data rather than executable code.

Output encoding is the practice of encoding or escaping user-generated content before rendering it in web pages.

This prevents injected scripts from executing in the user's browser and ensures that user input is treated as plain text.

Web application frameworks often provide built-in security mechanisms and libraries for input validation and output encoding, making it easier for developers to implement secure coding practices.

In summary, SQL injection and XSS testing are vital components of web application security assessments.

Regular testing, both automated and manual, helps identify and remediate vulnerabilities that could lead to data breaches, unauthorized access, or other security incidents.

Organizations must also prioritize secure coding practices, including input validation, parameterized queries, and output encoding, to prevent these vulnerabilities from arising in the first place.

By incorporating security testing into their development processes and fostering a culture of security awareness, organizations can reduce the risk of SQL injection and XSS vulnerabilities and better protect their web applications and users.

Chapter 7: Wireless Network Security

Wireless network enumeration is a critical phase in the realm of ethical hacking and network security, allowing professionals to discover and assess wireless networks within a given environment.

This process is essential for understanding the wireless landscape, identifying potential vulnerabilities, and enhancing the overall security of wireless networks.

Wireless network enumeration primarily involves the systematic scanning and probing of wireless access points (APs) and related infrastructure to gather information about their existence, configuration, and security posture.

One of the initial steps in wireless network enumeration is passive reconnaissance, which entails monitoring the surrounding area for wireless networks and APs without actively sending probing requests.

Tools like Wi-Fi scanners and wireless sniffers can be used to passively discover SSIDs (Service Set Identifiers) and assess the strength of wireless signals.

This information provides valuable insights into the physical layout of wireless networks, including the location of APs and potential coverage areas.

Active reconnaissance takes the process a step further by actively probing for wireless networks and APs.

This involves sending broadcast requests, such as probe requests, to elicit responses from nearby APs.

The responses typically include information about the APs, including their SSIDs, MAC addresses, signal strength, and supported encryption methods.

Active reconnaissance is a more direct approach that helps enumerate wireless networks more comprehensively.

War driving or war walking is a technique used in wireless network enumeration, involving the systematic scanning of an area while physically moving to detect and map wireless networks.

This approach is particularly useful for assessing the coverage and range of wireless networks in real-world environments.

Another aspect of wireless network enumeration is the identification of hidden or cloaked SSIDs, which are not broadcasted openly by APs.

Discovering hidden SSIDs requires the use of specialized tools that can send probe requests with specific SSID values to elicit responses from hidden networks.

Once wireless networks and APs have been enumerated, the next step is to assess their security posture and potential vulnerabilities.

Common vulnerabilities in wireless networks include weak encryption, default credentials, outdated firmware, and misconfigurations.

Security professionals often use tools and techniques to perform vulnerability scanning and penetration testing on wireless networks.

For example, tools like Aircrack-ng and Wifite are commonly used for cracking Wi-Fi passwords and performing dictionary attacks.

These tools simulate various attack scenarios to assess the security of wireless networks.

Additionally, security professionals may conduct rogue AP detection to identify unauthorized or malicious APs that could pose security risks.

Rogue APs can be used for attacks like man-in-the-middle (MitM) or evil twin attacks.

Wireless network enumeration is not limited to traditional Wi-Fi networks but also includes the assessment of other wireless technologies like Bluetooth, Zigbee, and cellular networks.

Each of these technologies has its own enumeration and security assessment methods.

For Bluetooth devices, enumeration may involve discovering and pairing with nearby Bluetooth devices to assess their security posture.

Enumeration of Zigbee networks may include scanning for Zigbee devices and assessing their configurations.

When it comes to cellular networks, enumeration may involve identifying nearby cell towers, capturing cellular traffic, and analyzing the security of cellular communications.

An essential aspect of wireless network enumeration is ensuring that the assessment is conducted legally and ethically.

Unauthorized access to wireless networks, probing, or interception of wireless communications can violate privacy laws and regulations.

Security professionals must obtain proper authorization from the network owner or administrator before conducting wireless network enumeration.

Moreover, ethical hackers must adhere to established rules of engagement and guidelines to ensure responsible and lawful testing.

In summary, wireless network enumeration is a crucial process in the field of ethical hacking and network security.

It involves the systematic discovery and assessment of wireless networks, access points, and related infrastructure to identify vulnerabilities and enhance security.

By conducting ethical and authorized wireless network enumeration, organizations can proactively identify and mitigate security risks in their wireless environments, safeguarding sensitive data and ensuring the confidentiality and integrity of their networks.

Mitigating wireless vulnerabilities is a critical aspect of maintaining the security and integrity of wireless networks in an increasingly connected world.

As wireless technologies continue to proliferate in both home and business environments, the need for effective mitigation strategies becomes paramount.

The first step in mitigating wireless vulnerabilities is to conduct a thorough assessment of the wireless network's security posture through techniques like wireless network enumeration and vulnerability scanning.

This assessment helps identify existing vulnerabilities, weaknesses, and potential attack vectors.

Once vulnerabilities are identified, organizations should prioritize remediation efforts based on the severity and potential impact of each vulnerability.

Common vulnerabilities in wireless networks include weak encryption protocols, default credentials, misconfigured access points, and rogue devices.

Addressing these vulnerabilities requires a combination of technical measures and best practices.

One fundamental mitigation strategy is to ensure strong encryption is in place for wireless communications.

Using modern encryption protocols like WPA3 for Wi-Fi networks helps protect data in transit and prevents eavesdropping.

Additionally, implementing strong, unique pre-shared keys (PSKs) or employing more secure authentication methods, such as EAP-TLS for enterprise networks, enhances wireless security.

Default credentials pose a significant risk in wireless networks, as attackers can exploit them to gain unauthorized access.

Mitigation involves changing default passwords and using strong, unique credentials for all wireless devices.

Regularly updating and patching firmware or software on wireless access points and devices is crucial.

Vendors often release updates to address security vulnerabilities, and staying current with these updates helps mitigate potential risks.

Another vital step is to disable unnecessary services and features on wireless access points.

By limiting the attack surface, organizations can reduce the potential for exploitation.

Additionally, organizations should configure access points and routers to use secure configurations and disable insecure protocols like WEP.

For enterprise networks, implementing robust authentication mechanisms, such as 802.1X with strong EAP methods, enhances security by ensuring that only authorized devices and users can access the network.

Employing network segmentation is another effective mitigation strategy.

Segmenting the network into separate VLANs or subnets isolates different types of traffic and reduces the lateral movement of attackers in the event of a breach.

Regularly monitoring wireless network traffic and using intrusion detection and prevention systems (IDS/IPS) help detect and block suspicious activities.

This includes monitoring for rogue access points and unauthorized devices.

Establishing a clear security policy for wireless networks is essential.

This policy should outline acceptable use, security measures, and guidelines for employees or users.

Training and educating employees about the risks associated with wireless networks and the importance of security best practices can help mitigate human error.

Physical security measures, such as locking server rooms and restricting physical access to wireless devices, are essential for preventing unauthorized tampering.

Implementing network monitoring and logging solutions enables organizations to track and investigate security incidents effectively.

In the event of a breach or suspicious activity, logs can provide valuable information for forensic analysis and incident response.

Creating an incident response plan specific to wireless network security helps organizations respond swiftly and effectively to security breaches.

The plan should outline steps for identifying, containing, and mitigating security incidents, as well as communicating with affected parties and authorities.

Wireless network security should be assessed regularly, including periodic vulnerability assessments and penetration testing.

These assessments help organizations identify emerging vulnerabilities and potential threats proactively.

Using specialized tools and techniques, ethical hackers can simulate real-world attacks to assess the network's resilience.

Regular assessments ensure that mitigation measures remain effective in the face of evolving threats.

In summary, mitigating wireless vulnerabilities is a multifaceted process that requires a combination of technical measures, best practices, and ongoing vigilance.

By implementing strong encryption, changing default credentials, patching devices, and following security policies and guidelines, organizations can reduce the risk of wireless attacks.

Network segmentation, monitoring, and incident response planning further enhance wireless security.

Continual assessment and proactive measures are key to maintaining the security and integrity of wireless networks in an ever-evolving threat landscape.

Chapter 8: Cloud Security and Auditing

Cloud computing has revolutionized the way organizations access and manage their IT resources, and at the heart of this transformation are the three primary cloud service models: Infrastructure as a Service (IaaS), Platform as a Service (PaaS), and Software as a Service (SaaS).

These service models provide businesses with a flexible and scalable approach to deploying and utilizing computing resources, allowing them to focus on their core activities while outsourcing the complexities of IT infrastructure management.

IaaS, which stands for Infrastructure as a Service, is a foundational cloud service model that provides organizations with virtualized computing resources over the internet.

With IaaS, businesses can rent virtual machines, storage, and networking components from cloud providers, eliminating the need to invest in and maintain physical hardware.

This model allows for greater flexibility and cost efficiency, as organizations can scale their infrastructure up or down based on demand.

PaaS, or Platform as a Service, takes cloud computing a step further by offering a comprehensive development and deployment environment in addition to infrastructure.

PaaS platforms provide tools, frameworks, and services that enable developers to build, test, and deploy applications without having to manage the underlying infrastructure.

This empowers development teams to focus on writing code and creating applications rather than dealing with the complexities of hardware provisioning and maintenance.

SaaS, short for Software as a Service, represents the highest level of abstraction in cloud computing.

In the SaaS model, software applications are delivered over the internet on a subscription basis.

Users can access these applications through web browsers or dedicated client software, and all maintenance, updates, and infrastructure management are handled by the SaaS provider.

This model offers unparalleled convenience for end-users, as they can access software from any device with an internet connection.

Each of these cloud service models has its own set of advantages and use cases.

IaaS is well-suited for organizations that require complete control over their virtualized infrastructure and want to leverage the cloud for scalable computing resources.

PaaS is ideal for development teams looking to streamline the application development and deployment process, reducing time-to-market and development costs.

SaaS, on the other hand, is an excellent choice for businesses seeking to eliminate the burden of software maintenance and upgrades while providing users with access to software from anywhere.

It's important to note that cloud service models are not mutually exclusive, and organizations often utilize a combination of these models to meet their specific needs.

For example, a company may use IaaS to host its virtual servers and storage, PaaS to develop and deploy custom applications, and SaaS for common productivity tools like email and office software.

Cloud service models offer several key benefits, including scalability, cost-efficiency, flexibility, and reduced IT management overhead.

Scalability is a fundamental advantage of cloud computing, as organizations can easily adjust their cloud resources to match changing demands.

This scalability enables businesses to handle traffic spikes, accommodate growth, and respond to fluctuations in demand without the need for large upfront investments in hardware.

Cost-efficiency is another significant benefit, as cloud service models allow organizations to pay only for the resources they consume, eliminating the need for capital expenditures on physical infrastructure.

The pay-as-you-go pricing model of cloud computing ensures that businesses can align their IT costs with actual usage.

Flexibility is a hallmark of cloud service models, enabling organizations to select the level of service that best suits their requirements.

This flexibility extends to the ability to choose between public, private, or hybrid cloud deployments, depending on security, compliance, and performance considerations.

Reduced IT management overhead is a key advantage for organizations that adopt cloud service models.

With IaaS, PaaS, and SaaS, cloud providers handle many of the administrative tasks associated with traditional IT operations, such as hardware maintenance, software updates, and security patching.

This allows IT teams to focus on strategic initiatives and innovation rather than routine maintenance tasks.

While cloud service models offer numerous advantages, they also introduce specific considerations and challenges.

Security and compliance are paramount concerns, particularly in public cloud deployments, as organizations must trust their cloud providers to protect sensitive data and adhere to regulatory requirements.

Performance and latency can be challenges in some cloud environments, particularly when dealing with data-intensive or real-time applications.

Vendor lock-in is a potential risk, as organizations may become dependent on specific cloud providers' proprietary technologies and APIs.

Additionally, cost management is essential, as cloud costs can escalate if resources are not properly monitored and optimized.

In summary, cloud service models - IaaS, PaaS, and SaaS - represent the foundation of modern cloud computing, offering organizations the flexibility, scalability, and cost-efficiency needed to meet their IT requirements.

While each model has its unique advantages and use cases, many organizations leverage a combination of these models to achieve their specific goals.

It is crucial for businesses to carefully evaluate their cloud computing needs, consider the benefits and challenges of each service model, and select the approach that aligns best with their strategic objectives.

Securing cloud-based environments is a paramount concern for organizations as they increasingly rely on cloud services to store, process, and manage their data and applications.

The shift to the cloud offers numerous advantages, including scalability, flexibility, and cost-efficiency, but it also introduces unique security challenges that require careful consideration and proactive measures.

One of the first steps in securing cloud-based environments is understanding the shared responsibility model, which delineates the security responsibilities between cloud service providers and customers.

In a shared responsibility model, the cloud provider is responsible for securing the underlying infrastructure, including the physical data centers, networking, and hypervisors.

On the other hand, customers are responsible for securing their data, applications, configurations, and access controls within the cloud environment.

This division of responsibilities underscores the need for organizations to implement robust security practices and controls within their cloud instances.

Identity and access management (IAM) is a foundational component of cloud security, enabling organizations to control who has access to their cloud resources and what actions they can perform.

Implementing strong IAM practices, such as role-based access control (RBAC) and multi-factor authentication (MFA), helps prevent unauthorized access and potential breaches.

Additionally, organizations should regularly review and audit IAM policies to ensure that access permissions remain aligned with business requirements.

Data encryption plays a crucial role in securing data within cloud-based environments.

Data at rest and in transit should be encrypted to protect against data breaches and unauthorized access.

Cloud providers often offer encryption services, and organizations should take advantage of these features to safeguard their sensitive information.

Moreover, organizations should manage encryption keys securely to prevent unauthorized access to encrypted data.

Monitoring and logging are essential for detecting and responding to security incidents in cloud environments.

Organizations should implement robust monitoring solutions that capture logs and events from their cloud resources.

These logs can provide valuable insights into user activities, resource changes, and potential security threats.

Security information and event management (SIEM) tools can help centralize and analyze these logs, allowing organizations to identify anomalies and respond to incidents promptly.

Regular vulnerability assessments and penetration testing are critical for identifying and mitigating security weaknesses in cloud environments.

These assessments should cover both the cloud infrastructure and the applications hosted within the cloud.

By proactively identifying vulnerabilities, organizations can address them before they are exploited by attackers.

Configuration management and security baselining are fundamental practices for ensuring that cloud resources are properly configured and secure.

Organizations should establish security baselines for their cloud instances and regularly assess configurations against these baselines.

Automated configuration management tools can help enforce security policies and ensure that resources adhere to best practices.

Network security within cloud environments requires careful attention.

Organizations should implement network segmentation and firewall rules to control traffic flow and prevent lateral movement by attackers.

Additionally, cloud security groups or network security groups should be used to restrict access to resources based on predefined rules.

Threat detection and incident response capabilities are essential for rapidly identifying and mitigating security threats in cloud environments.

Organizations should deploy intrusion detection systems (IDS) and intrusion prevention systems (IPS) to monitor network traffic for suspicious activities and respond to threats in real-time.

Cloud providers offer various security services and features that organizations can leverage to enhance their cloud security.

For example, AWS offers services like AWS Identity and Access Management (IAM), Amazon GuardDuty for threat detection, and AWS Config for configuration management.

Microsoft Azure provides Azure Active Directory for identity and access management and Azure Security Center for threat detection and response.

Google Cloud Platform offers Google Cloud Identity and Access Management (IAM) and Google Cloud Security Command Center for security monitoring.

It is essential for organizations to stay informed about the security services and features offered by their chosen cloud provider and use them effectively.

Compliance with industry regulations and data protection laws is a critical aspect of cloud security.

Organizations must ensure that their cloud environment complies with relevant regulations, such as the General Data Protection Regulation (GDPR), the Health Insurance Portability and Accountability Act (HIPAA), and the Payment Card Industry Data Security Standard (PCI DSS).

Cloud providers often offer compliance certifications and tools to assist customers in meeting these requirements.

Finally, ongoing security awareness and training for employees are essential.

Employees should be educated about security best practices, the risks associated with cloud computing, and how to recognize and report security incidents.

Organizations can conduct security awareness programs and provide regular training to help employees stay vigilant and informed.

In summary, securing cloud-based environments is a multifaceted endeavor that requires a combination of technical controls, best practices, and ongoing vigilance.

Organizations should embrace the shared responsibility model, implement strong identity and access management, encrypt data, monitor for security threats, and regularly assess and test their cloud security posture.

By taking a proactive approach to cloud security, organizations can enjoy the benefits of cloud computing while minimizing security risks and protecting their data and resources.

Chapter 9: Insider Threat Detection

Insider threats are a significant concern for organizations, as they involve individuals within the organization who pose a security risk due to their access to sensitive data, systems, and resources.

Identifying insider threat indicators is crucial for early detection and mitigation of potential security breaches.

Insider threat indicators encompass a wide range of behaviors, actions, and patterns that may suggest malicious or harmful intent by an employee, contractor, or other trusted entity.

One common indicator is a sudden change in behavior, such as an employee becoming disgruntled or displaying signs of discontent.

This change in behavior may manifest as increased absenteeism, declining job performance, or conflicts with colleagues.

Another insider threat indicator is excessive access to sensitive data or systems beyond an individual's role or responsibilities.

Unauthorized access to confidential information can be a strong indicator of malicious intent or data theft.

In some cases, insiders may attempt to cover their tracks by using unauthorized methods or exploiting vulnerabilities to gain access to data or systems.

For instance, an insider may use stolen or compromised credentials to bypass security controls.

Insiders may also exhibit unusual or suspicious online behavior, such as accessing prohibited websites, engaging in unauthorized file downloads, or sharing sensitive information via unapproved channels.

Monitoring and analyzing network traffic and user activities can help detect these indicators.

Changes in an individual's financial situation may also be indicative of an insider threat.

For example, an employee experiencing financial difficulties may be more susceptible to offers of financial gain in exchange for insider information or access.

Additionally, employees who engage in unauthorized or unexplained external communications, especially with competitors or malicious actors, can raise suspicions.

Insiders may attempt to communicate with external entities to share sensitive information or coordinate malicious activities.

Another important indicator is the misuse of privileged access.

Employees with elevated privileges, such as system administrators or database administrators, may abuse their access to steal data, tamper with systems, or disrupt operations.

Insider threats may escalate their activities over time, starting with low-level security violations and gradually increasing their malicious actions.

This progression can include activities like password sharing, unauthorized data access, and ultimately, data exfiltration or system sabotage.

Employee dissatisfaction, perceived unfair treatment, or a desire for revenge can also contribute to insider threats.

Individuals who feel wronged by the organization may seek to harm it by leaking sensitive information, damaging systems, or disrupting operations.

Detection of insider threat indicators often relies on a combination of technology, monitoring, and behavioral analysis.

User behavior analytics (UBA) tools can help identify unusual patterns of behavior that may indicate insider threats.

These tools analyze user activities, log data, and network traffic to detect deviations from normal behavior.

Insiders may attempt to cover their tracks or hide their activities, making it essential to implement advanced threat detection and monitoring solutions.

Organizations should also establish clear and comprehensive insider threat detection policies and procedures.

These policies should define what constitutes insider threats, how they will be investigated, and the consequences for individuals found guilty of insider misconduct.

Regular security awareness training and education for employees can help them recognize potential insider threat indicators and understand the importance of reporting suspicious activities.

Creating a culture of trust and openness, where employees feel comfortable reporting concerns without fear of retaliation, is essential.

Organizations should implement a robust incident response plan specifically tailored to address insider threats.

This plan should outline steps for investigating suspected insider threats, preserving evidence, and taking appropriate actions, including legal and HR measures.

Collaboration between IT, security, and HR departments is vital in addressing insider threats effectively.

In summary, insider threat indicators encompass various behaviors, actions, and patterns that may suggest malicious intent or misconduct by individuals within an organization.

Detecting and mitigating insider threats requires a combination of technology, monitoring, policies, and employee education.

Early detection and proactive measures are essential for protecting sensitive data, systems, and resources from insider threats and minimizing the potential impact of security breaches.

Behavioral analytics and user monitoring are essential components of modern cybersecurity strategies, offering organizations powerful tools for identifying and mitigating security threats.

These approaches focus on understanding the behavior of users and entities within an organization's network to detect deviations from normal patterns that may indicate malicious activity.

Behavioral analytics leverages advanced algorithms and machine learning to analyze vast amounts of data, including user activity logs, network traffic, and system events.

By establishing a baseline of normal behavior for users and entities, these systems can identify anomalies that may signify security incidents.

User monitoring, on the other hand, involves the continuous observation of user activities, including login and logoff times, file access, application usage, and communication patterns.

By closely tracking these activities, organizations can promptly detect any unusual behavior that could indicate a security breach or insider threat.

Behavioral analytics and user monitoring are particularly valuable in the context of insider threats, where individuals within an organization may pose a security risk.

Insider threats can manifest in various ways, from employees with malicious intent seeking to steal sensitive data to unintentional actions that may compromise security.

One common type of insider threat is data exfiltration, where employees attempt to steal and transmit confidential information outside the organization.

Behavioral analytics can detect unusual data transfer patterns or unauthorized access to sensitive files, triggering alerts for further investigation.

Additionally, insider threats may involve employees intentionally or unintentionally disclosing sensitive information through unauthorized channels, such as email or file sharing services.

User monitoring can identify and flag suspicious communication patterns or file sharing activities that deviate from established norms.

Unauthorized access to systems or data is another insider threat scenario that behavioral analytics and user monitoring can address.

When users with legitimate access credentials attempt to access resources beyond their usual scope, these tools can identify the anomaly and alert security teams.

Insiders with malicious intent may escalate their activities over time, starting with seemingly minor security violations, such as sharing passwords or accessing restricted files.

By closely monitoring user behavior, organizations can detect these early warning signs and intervene before the situation escalates further.

Behavioral analytics and user monitoring are not limited to insider threats; they are also valuable for identifying external threats, such as cyberattacks.

Advanced persistent threats (APTs) and other sophisticated attacks often involve attackers moving stealthily within a network, mimicking legitimate user behavior to avoid detection.

Behavioral analytics can identify unusual patterns of network traffic or system access, which may indicate an ongoing cyberattack.

Furthermore, user monitoring can track the activities of privileged users, such as system administrators, who may inadvertently or intentionally take actions that compromise security.

By closely observing the behavior of these users, organizations can ensure that they adhere to established security protocols.

Implementing behavioral analytics and user monitoring involves several key steps.

First, organizations must define and establish baselines for normal user behavior and network activities.

This baseline serves as a reference point against which deviations can be identified.

Once the baseline is established, organizations can deploy behavioral analytics solutions that continuously monitor user and entity behavior.

These solutions employ machine learning algorithms to analyze data, detect anomalies, and generate alerts when suspicious activities are identified.

It is essential to integrate behavioral analytics with existing security systems, such as intrusion detection and prevention systems (IDS/IPS), security information and event management (SIEM) tools, and threat intelligence feeds.

This integration enhances the organization's ability to correlate and analyze data from multiple sources, providing a comprehensive view of security threats.

User monitoring involves the collection and analysis of user activity data, which may include logins, file access, email communications, and application usage.

Organizations can employ user monitoring tools and log analysis solutions to capture and analyze this data.

Furthermore, user monitoring should be part of a broader security awareness program that educates employees about the importance of security policies, the risks of insider threats, and the consequences of security violations.

Creating a culture of security awareness encourages employees to adhere to security best practices and report any suspicious activities they may encounter.

Regularly reviewing and refining the security policies and access controls in place is essential for maintaining the effectiveness of behavioral analytics and user monitoring.

Security policies should be updated to reflect changes in the threat landscape and the organization's evolving security requirements.

Additionally, organizations should conduct periodic assessments of their behavioral analytics and user monitoring practices to identify areas for improvement and optimization.

In summary, behavioral analytics and user monitoring are indispensable tools for identifying and mitigating security threats, including insider threats and external cyberattacks.

By continuously monitoring user behavior and network activities, organizations can detect anomalies, unusual patterns, and deviations from normal behavior, enabling them to respond promptly to security incidents.

These approaches contribute to a proactive cybersecurity strategy that enhances an organization's overall security posture and reduces the risks associated with insider threats and sophisticated cyberattacks.

Chapter 10: Post-Audit Reporting and Remediation

Documentation and reporting are integral aspects of effective cybersecurity practices, providing organizations with the means to record, analyze, and communicate critical information related to security incidents, policies, procedures, and compliance.

In the realm of cybersecurity, documentation serves as a foundational element that supports various security functions, such as incident response, risk management, compliance, and the establishment of security policies and procedures.

Documentation encompasses a wide range of artifacts, including security policies, procedures, guidelines, standards, and records.

These documents serve as the blueprint for an organization's security posture, outlining the principles, practices, and controls necessary to protect its information assets and infrastructure.

Security policies define the overarching principles and objectives of an organization's security program, outlining its commitment to safeguarding sensitive data, systems, and resources.

These policies establish the framework for security practices and set the tone for the organization's security culture.

Security procedures, on the other hand, provide detailed, step-by-step instructions for implementing security controls and responding to specific security incidents.

These procedures guide employees and security professionals in carrying out security-related tasks and actions systematically.

Guidelines and standards complement security policies and procedures by offering specific recommendations, best practices, and technical requirements for achieving security objectives.

Documentation also plays a critical role in risk management by helping organizations identify, assess, and mitigate security risks.

Risk assessments and risk management plans are essential documents that enable organizations to evaluate their vulnerabilities, threats, and potential impacts on their information assets.

These documents inform decision-makers about the prioritization of security measures and resource allocation to address identified risks effectively.

Furthermore, documentation supports compliance efforts by providing a record of security controls, policies, and practices that align with industry regulations, standards, and legal requirements.

Compliance documentation demonstrates an organization's commitment to adhering to specific security mandates and provides evidence of its adherence during audits and assessments.

Security records are a crucial component of documentation, serving as the historical record of security incidents, activities, and changes within an organization's environment.

These records include incident reports, audit logs, vulnerability assessments, and configuration change records.

In the event of a security incident, incident reports document the details of the event, including the nature of the incident, its impact, the actions taken to mitigate it, and lessons learned.

Audit logs provide a chronological record of system and user activities, enabling organizations to trace security events and detect unauthorized or suspicious activities.

Vulnerability assessments and configuration change records help organizations track changes made to their systems, applications, and network infrastructure.

Effectively managing and organizing documentation is crucial for maintaining the integrity and accessibility of security information.

Document repositories and management systems facilitate the creation, storage, retrieval, and version control of security documents.

Organizations should establish clear document retention and disposal policies to ensure that documents are retained for the necessary period and securely disposed of when they are no longer needed.

Reporting is an essential aspect of documentation, enabling organizations to communicate key security information to various stakeholders, including executives, employees, auditors, and regulatory bodies.

Security reports provide insights into the organization's security posture, incident response activities, compliance status, and overall security effectiveness.

Executive reports offer a high-level view of the organization's security posture, summarizing key security metrics, risks, and incidents in a format that is easily digestible by senior leadership.

These reports help executives make informed decisions and allocate resources to address security concerns effectively.

Operational reports provide detailed information about security incidents, vulnerabilities, and activities within the organization's security operations center (SOC) or incident response team.

These reports enable security professionals to monitor and respond to security events in real-time, ensuring a proactive security stance.

Compliance reports are essential for demonstrating adherence to industry regulations, standards, and legal requirements.

These reports are often required for regulatory audits and assessments and provide evidence of the organization's commitment to security compliance.

Security awareness and training reports help track the progress and effectiveness of security education programs within the organization.

These reports inform security leaders about employee participation, completion rates, and areas that may require additional training or awareness initiatives.

In summary, documentation and reporting are fundamental to an organization's cybersecurity efforts, providing the structure, records, and communication necessary to establish and maintain an effective security program.

Well-documented security policies, procedures, and guidelines set the foundation for security practices, while records and reports help organizations manage risks, demonstrate compliance, and respond to security incidents effectively.

By maintaining comprehensive and organized documentation and reporting practices, organizations can enhance their security posture, mitigate risks, and protect their valuable information assets.

Effective remediation strategies are a critical component of cybersecurity programs, as they play a central role in identifying, addressing, and mitigating security vulnerabilities and incidents.

These strategies are designed to respond to security incidents promptly, minimize their impact, and prevent their recurrence.

One of the fundamental principles of effective remediation is the timely identification of security issues, which requires robust monitoring and alerting systems that can detect suspicious activities and anomalies within an organization's network and systems.

Once a security issue is identified, organizations must prioritize it based on its severity, potential impact, and the likelihood of exploitation.

Prioritization enables organizations to allocate resources and address the most critical issues first, reducing the overall risk exposure.

Effective remediation strategies should involve a well-defined incident response process that outlines the steps to be taken when a security incident is detected.

This process typically includes identification, containment, eradication, recovery, and lessons learned phases.

Identification involves confirming the presence of an incident, understanding its scope, and assessing the potential impact.

Containment aims to prevent the incident from spreading further and causing additional harm, often by isolating affected systems or network segments.

Eradication focuses on completely removing the root cause of the incident, eliminating any malware or unauthorized access, and patching vulnerabilities.

Recovery involves restoring affected systems and services to normal operation, often with the help of backups and tested recovery procedures.

The lessons learned phase is crucial for continuous improvement, as it involves analyzing the incident to identify root causes, vulnerabilities, and areas for process or technology enhancements.

Another key element of effective remediation strategies is the use of security controls and technologies to aid in incident response.

These controls may include intrusion detection and prevention systems (IDS/IPS), firewalls, antivirus software, and security information and event management (SIEM) solutions.

Security teams should leverage these technologies to detect, block, and respond to security threats in real-time.

Regular vulnerability assessments and penetration testing can also help organizations proactively identify and remediate vulnerabilities before they are exploited.

Effective communication and collaboration are essential during the remediation process, as they facilitate coordination among IT teams, security professionals, and other stakeholders.

Clear communication ensures that everyone is aware of their roles and responsibilities, reducing the risk of missteps or delays in incident response.

Documentation is a critical aspect of effective remediation, as it provides a record of the incident, actions taken, and lessons learned.

Documentation helps organizations improve their incident response processes, share knowledge, and maintain a historical record of security incidents for future reference.

Additionally, organizations should establish incident response playbooks and runbooks that outline step-by-step procedures for various types of incidents.

These playbooks help ensure a consistent and efficient response to security incidents, even in high-pressure situations.

Effective remediation strategies should also involve continuous monitoring and testing of security controls and incident response processes.

Organizations should regularly assess the effectiveness of their security measures and incident response capabilities through tabletop exercises, red teaming, and incident simulation exercises.

These activities help identify weaknesses, evaluate the readiness of the organization, and provide opportunities for improvement.

Security professionals should stay informed about emerging threats, vulnerabilities, and attack techniques to adapt their remediation strategies accordingly.

Threat intelligence feeds, security forums, and industry publications are valuable sources of information for understanding the evolving threat landscape.

Furthermore, organizations should implement a strong security patch management process to address vulnerabilities promptly.

This process includes identifying, prioritizing, testing, and applying patches to systems and software.

Patch management helps reduce the attack surface by closing known security holes.

Effective remediation also involves proactive measures to enhance security posture, such as implementing defense-in-depth strategies, network segmentation, and robust access controls.

These measures can help prevent security incidents and reduce the potential impact when incidents do occur.

In summary, effective remediation strategies are essential for organizations to respond to security incidents, vulnerabilities, and emerging threats effectively.

These strategies encompass timely identification, prioritization, incident response processes, security controls, communication, documentation, continuous monitoring, and proactive security measures.

By implementing comprehensive remediation strategies and continuously improving incident response capabilities, organizations can better protect their information assets and minimize the impact of security incidents.

BOOK 2
BEYOND THE BASICS
ADVANCED SECURITY AUDITING FOR ETHICAL HACKERS

ROB BOTWRIGHT

Chapter 1: Deep Dive into Ethical Hacking

Understanding ethical hacking fundamentals is essential for individuals and organizations seeking to protect their digital assets and infrastructure from cyber threats.

Ethical hacking, also known as penetration testing or white-hat hacking, is a proactive approach to identifying vulnerabilities in computer systems, networks, and applications by simulating real-world cyberattacks.

Ethical hackers, often referred to as penetration testers or security professionals, use their skills and knowledge to assess the security of an organization's systems and provide recommendations for remediation.

To comprehend the fundamentals of ethical hacking, one must first grasp the concept of hacking itself.

Hacking refers to the unauthorized access, manipulation, or exploitation of computer systems and data with malicious intent.

However, ethical hacking diverges from malicious hacking in its purpose and legality.

Ethical hackers operate with the explicit permission of the system's owner to identify and rectify security weaknesses.

The primary goal of ethical hacking is to help organizations improve their security posture and protect against potential cyber threats.

Ethical hackers follow a code of ethics and legal guidelines, ensuring that their activities are conducted transparently, lawfully, and with the utmost integrity.

Ethical hacking encompasses a broad spectrum of techniques and methodologies that security professionals employ to assess an organization's security.

One of the fundamental methodologies in ethical hacking is reconnaissance, which involves gathering information about the target system, network, or application.

Reconnaissance aims to identify potential vulnerabilities, such as open ports, publicly accessible information, and potential attack vectors.

The information gathered during reconnaissance serves as a foundation for planning and executing ethical hacking tests.

Ethical hackers often utilize various scanning and enumeration tools to identify vulnerabilities and misconfigurations within a target environment.

These tools help assess the security posture of the target system and provide insights into potential weaknesses.

Vulnerability assessment is another critical aspect of ethical hacking, involving the systematic identification and evaluation of vulnerabilities.

Ethical hackers use vulnerability scanning tools to search for known vulnerabilities within the target systems, applications, and network devices.

Once vulnerabilities are identified, they are categorized based on severity and potential impact to prioritize remediation efforts.

The next phase of ethical hacking involves exploitation, where ethical hackers attempt to exploit identified vulnerabilities to gain unauthorized access or control over the target system.

This phase simulates real-world attacks and helps organizations understand the potential risks associated with unpatched or misconfigured systems.

Exploitation may involve techniques such as buffer overflows, SQL injection, or social engineering, depending on the vulnerabilities discovered.

While ethical hackers aim to exploit vulnerabilities, they do so with caution and within the boundaries defined by the engagement's scope.

Ethical hacking engagements often include rules of engagement and scope documents that outline the permissible activities and targets.

Post-exploitation activities include maintaining access to the compromised system, escalating privileges, and documenting the steps taken.

These activities help ethical hackers assess the potential damage that could occur if an attacker were to successfully exploit the vulnerabilities.

Another vital component of ethical hacking is reporting and documentation.

Ethical hackers document their findings, including the vulnerabilities discovered, the steps taken to exploit them, and the potential impact of successful attacks.

A comprehensive report is then provided to the organization, detailing the security weaknesses and recommended remediation measures.

Clear and concise reporting is crucial to ensure that organizations can prioritize and address identified vulnerabilities effectively.

Ethical hackers must possess a deep understanding of various operating systems, networking protocols, and programming languages to be effective in their assessments.

They often have certifications such as Certified Ethical Hacker (CEH) or Offensive Security Certified Professional (OSCP) to demonstrate their expertise.

Additionally, ethical hackers stay updated on the latest security threats, vulnerabilities, and attack techniques through continuous learning and professional development.

Ethical hacking is not a one-time activity but an ongoing process that helps organizations maintain a strong security posture in the face of evolving threats.

Organizations should consider conducting regular ethical hacking assessments, known as penetration tests or security audits, to proactively identify and address security weaknesses.

By understanding the fundamentals of ethical hacking and embracing it as a crucial element of their cybersecurity strategy, organizations can better protect their digital assets and data from cyber threats.

Legal and ethical considerations are paramount in the field of ethical hacking, as they define the boundaries and responsibilities of security professionals who engage in penetration testing and vulnerability assessments.

Ethical hackers must adhere to a strict code of ethics to ensure that their actions align with both the law and accepted ethical principles.

One of the fundamental ethical principles in ethical hacking is obtaining explicit and written authorization from the organization or individual that owns or operates the target systems.

Without proper authorization, conducting penetration tests or security assessments can be considered illegal and unethical.

Authorization should be well-documented and specify the scope, rules of engagement, and objectives of the ethical hacking engagement.

Additionally, ethical hackers must operate within the boundaries defined by the authorization, refraining from any actions that could cause harm, disruption, or unauthorized access beyond the agreed-upon scope.

Unauthorized access to computer systems, networks, or data is not only illegal but also a breach of ethical standards.

To ensure compliance with the law, ethical hackers should be well-versed in relevant cybersecurity regulations, data protection laws, and intellectual property rights.

Privacy laws, such as the General Data Protection Regulation (GDPR) and the Health Insurance Portability and Accountability Act (HIPAA), have specific requirements for handling and protecting sensitive data during security assessments.

Ethical hackers must respect these legal obligations and ensure that they do not violate the privacy rights of individuals or organizations.

Furthermore, ethical hackers should maintain strict confidentiality and nondisclosure agreements to protect the sensitive information they may encounter during assessments.

Unauthorized disclosure of confidential information, trade secrets, or proprietary data can have severe legal and ethical consequences.

Transparency and honesty are foundational principles in ethical hacking, as ethical hackers are expected to provide truthful and accurate information about their findings.

Misrepresenting or exaggerating the severity of vulnerabilities, as well as withholding critical information, can harm an organization's security posture and credibility.

Ethical hackers should prioritize clear and comprehensive reporting, detailing the vulnerabilities discovered, the potential impact of successful exploits, and recommended remediation measures.

When conducting ethical hacking assessments, it is crucial to avoid causing unnecessary harm or disruption to the target systems or network.

Ethical hackers should exercise caution and restraint, taking steps to minimize the risk of unintended consequences or collateral damage.

They should be prepared to halt their activities immediately if any unexpected issues arise.

Moreover, ethical hackers should engage in responsible disclosure when they discover vulnerabilities.

This involves notifying the affected organization of the security weaknesses and providing a reasonable timeframe for remediation before disclosing the findings publicly.

Responsible disclosure helps organizations address vulnerabilities without exposing themselves to unnecessary risks.

Another ethical consideration in ethical hacking is the principle of non-interference with critical infrastructure or systems that could jeopardize public safety.

Ethical hackers should avoid targeting systems such as power grids, healthcare equipment, or transportation systems that could have life-threatening consequences if disrupted.

Engaging in activities that could harm public safety is not only unethical but also illegal.

Furthermore, ethical hackers must respect the intellectual property rights of others, including copyrights, patents, and trademarks.

Using or distributing copyrighted materials without proper authorization is both unethical and illegal.

Ethical hackers should ensure that they have the legal right to use any tools, software, or resources during their assessments and respect the intellectual property of tool developers and organizations.

A critical aspect of ethical hacking is ongoing professional development and education to stay informed about changes in the legal and ethical landscape.

Laws and regulations related to cybersecurity and privacy can evolve rapidly, and ethical hackers must adapt their practices accordingly.

Participating in training, obtaining certifications, and staying informed about legal developments are essential steps in maintaining ethical standards.

Moreover, ethical hackers should seek legal counsel or guidance when navigating complex legal and ethical issues.

Consulting with legal experts can help ensure that their activities align with the law and ethical standards.

In summary, legal and ethical considerations are integral to the practice of ethical hacking, guiding the actions and responsibilities of security professionals who assess the security of systems and networks.

Ethical hackers must obtain proper authorization, respect privacy and data protection laws, maintain confidentiality, practice transparency, and avoid causing harm or disrupting critical infrastructure.

Adhering to legal and ethical principles is not only a professional responsibility but also a fundamental requirement for conducting ethical hacking assessments responsibly and effectively.

Chapter 2: Advanced Reconnaissance Techniques

OSINT (Open Source Intelligence) gathering is a crucial aspect of modern cybersecurity and investigative work, providing valuable insights from publicly available information sources.

This practice involves the systematic collection, analysis, and interpretation of data from open and publicly accessible sources, such as websites, social media, online forums, news articles, and government publications.

OSINT gathering is a legitimate and legal method for acquiring information, as it relies solely on publicly accessible data.

One of the primary goals of OSINT gathering is to gather relevant information about individuals, organizations, or specific topics to assess potential security risks, vulnerabilities, or threats.

OSINT practitioners use a variety of tools and techniques to gather and analyze data effectively, and the information obtained can be used for a wide range of purposes, including cybersecurity, threat intelligence, law enforcement, and business intelligence.

Understanding the fundamentals of OSINT gathering is essential for security professionals, investigators, and analysts to enhance their ability to collect and leverage publicly available data effectively.

The process of OSINT gathering begins with defining the scope and objectives of the investigation or analysis, which helps identify the specific information needed and the sources to be examined.

Once the scope is defined, OSINT practitioners conduct systematic searches on the internet, utilizing search engines, specialized OSINT tools, and social media platforms to gather relevant data.

Web scraping and data extraction techniques may also be employed to automate the collection of information from websites and online databases.

Social media platforms play a significant role in OSINT gathering, as they often contain a wealth of information about individuals, organizations, and current events.

OSINT practitioners monitor social media accounts, posts, comments, and profiles to gather insights, trends, and potential indicators of security threats or vulnerabilities.

Online forums and discussion boards are valuable sources of information, as they provide discussions and conversations on various topics, including cybersecurity, technology, and current events.

By monitoring these forums, OSINT gatherers can identify emerging trends, discussions related to vulnerabilities, and potential threat actors.

News articles and publications from reputable sources can provide critical insights into current events, cybersecurity incidents, and the activities of organizations or individuals.

OSINT practitioners regularly review news articles and publications to stay informed and extract relevant information for their investigations.

Government websites and public records are often overlooked but can be rich sources of data, including business registrations, licenses, court records, and regulatory filings.

OSINT practitioners may access government databases to retrieve valuable information related to their investigations.

Online tools and platforms specifically designed for OSINT gathering can simplify the process by aggregating data from multiple sources, automating searches, and presenting the information in a structured format.

These tools may include search engines tailored for OSINT, domain and IP address analysis tools, and social media monitoring platforms.

Geolocation data, including IP addresses and GPS coordinates, can provide insights into the physical location of individuals or organizations.

OSINT practitioners may use geolocation tools to map and analyze the locations associated with specific online activities or threats.

When conducting OSINT gathering, it is essential to maintain ethical and legal boundaries.

OSINT practitioners should adhere to ethical guidelines and respect privacy, avoiding intrusive or malicious activities.

Additionally, practitioners should be aware of copyright and intellectual property laws when collecting and using publicly available data.

While OSINT gathering focuses on open and publicly accessible sources, it is essential to verify the accuracy and reliability of the information collected.

Cross-referencing data from multiple sources and evaluating the credibility of the sources themselves are crucial steps in ensuring the quality of OSINT findings.

Collaboration and information sharing among OSINT practitioners and the broader cybersecurity and intelligence communities can enhance the effectiveness of OSINT efforts.

By sharing insights, best practices, and emerging threats, OSINT professionals can collectively improve their ability to identify and respond to security risks.

In summary, OSINT gathering is a vital component of modern cybersecurity and investigative work, enabling practitioners to harness publicly available data for a variety of purposes.

Understanding the fundamentals of OSINT gathering, including defining scope, utilizing tools and techniques, respecting ethical and legal boundaries, and verifying information, is essential for security professionals and investigators to enhance their capabilities in collecting and leveraging open source intelligence.

Footprinting and information enumeration are crucial initial phases in the reconnaissance process of ethical hacking, allowing security professionals to gather essential data about a target, identify potential vulnerabilities, and assess the organization's security posture.

These phases provide a foundation for subsequent ethical hacking activities, helping practitioners develop a comprehensive understanding of the target's digital footprint.

Footprinting involves the systematic collection of data about a target, including its network infrastructure, IP addresses, domain names, and publicly accessible systems and services.

The goal of footprinting is to create a comprehensive map of the target's online presence, which is instrumental in identifying potential entry points for attackers and understanding the organization's attack surface.

Information enumeration, on the other hand, focuses on gathering specific details about the target's systems, devices, and applications.

This phase involves identifying active hosts, open ports, and services running on those hosts, along with information about the operating systems, software versions, and configurations in use.

By combining footprinting and information enumeration, ethical hackers can create a detailed profile of the target, helping them develop tailored attack strategies and prioritize potential vulnerabilities.

The process of footprinting begins with passive reconnaissance, where practitioners collect publicly available information about the target without directly interacting with its systems.

Passive reconnaissance may involve searching for the target's domain names, email addresses, and employee names on search engines, social media platforms, and public directories.

This phase can yield valuable information such as email addresses, employee roles, and potentially sensitive data that might be exposed unintentionally.

Social engineering tactics may also be employed during passive reconnaissance to gather information from employees, contractors, or partners.

By posing as a trusted individual or organization, ethical hackers can elicit information about the target's systems, technologies, and infrastructure.

Another critical aspect of footprinting is DNS enumeration, which involves querying DNS (Domain Name System) servers to discover domain names, subdomains, and associated IP addresses belonging to the target organization.

DNS enumeration can unveil valuable information about the target's network topology and the services it provides.

Subdomain discovery is a specific DNS enumeration technique that focuses on identifying subdomains associated with the target's primary domain.

Subdomains can provide insights into the organization's internal structure and the services it offers to the public.

WHOIS lookup is another useful technique in footprinting, allowing practitioners to obtain information about domain names, including registration details, administrative contacts, and expiration dates.

WHOIS data can provide valuable insights into the organization's ownership, affiliations, and historical changes.

Active reconnaissance is the next phase in footprinting, involving direct interactions with the target's systems and services to collect additional information.

Port scanning is a fundamental active reconnaissance technique, where ethical hackers use specialized tools to probe a target's network for open ports and services.

Port scanning helps identify which services are running on which hosts, providing a clearer picture of the target's infrastructure.

Banner grabbing is often performed in conjunction with port scanning, as it allows practitioners to retrieve information about the version and configuration of services running on open ports.

Banner grabbing can help identify potential vulnerabilities associated with specific service versions.

In addition to port scanning, ethical hackers may use traceroute or path analysis tools to map the network paths between their system and the target.

Traceroute provides insights into the network topology, helping practitioners understand the routes data packets take when traveling between hosts.

Furthermore, operating system fingerprinting is an essential aspect of information enumeration, enabling ethical hackers to identify the operating systems running on the target's hosts.

This information is crucial for tailoring subsequent attacks and selecting appropriate exploits.

By combining the results of DNS enumeration, port scanning, banner grabbing, and operating system fingerprinting, ethical hackers can create a detailed footprint of the target organization's digital infrastructure.

Information enumeration goes beyond the network level, delving into the specifics of target systems, applications, and services.

This phase may involve vulnerability scanning, where ethical hackers use specialized tools to identify potential vulnerabilities in the target's systems.

Vulnerability scanning helps prioritize potential weaknesses that could be exploited in subsequent ethical hacking activities.

Enumeration techniques also include service enumeration, which involves identifying active services on target hosts and collecting detailed information about those services.

This phase helps ethical hackers understand the functionalities, configurations, and potential vulnerabilities associated with specific services.

Similarly, network enumeration focuses on identifying network devices, including routers, switches, and firewalls, to gain insights into the target's network architecture.

Additionally, SNMP (Simple Network Management Protocol) enumeration may be employed to retrieve information about network devices and their configurations.

Web enumeration techniques aim to uncover information about web applications and websites hosted by the target.

This includes identifying web servers, web technologies, and potentially sensitive directories or files that may be exposed.

By understanding the target's web presence, ethical hackers can assess potential attack vectors related to web applications.

Directory and file enumeration, often performed through tools like directory brute-forcing, helps uncover hidden or unprotected resources on web servers.

Enumeration techniques also extend to email systems, where ethical hackers may attempt to identify valid email addresses, distribution lists, and mail server configurations.

This information can be valuable for future social engineering attacks or email-based exploits.

Overall, footprinting and information enumeration are essential phases in ethical hacking, allowing practitioners to collect critical data about the target organization's digital footprint, network topology, system configurations, and potential vulnerabilities.

These phases serve as the foundation for subsequent ethical hacking activities, enabling practitioners to develop tailored attack strategies and prioritize security assessments effectively.

Chapter 3: Exploiting Security Vulnerabilities

Identifying and exploiting common weaknesses is a fundamental aspect of ethical hacking, as it allows security professionals to uncover vulnerabilities and weaknesses in systems, applications, and networks before malicious hackers can exploit them.

Common weaknesses encompass a wide range of security issues, from misconfigurations and poor password practices to software vulnerabilities and social engineering techniques.

One of the first steps in identifying common weaknesses is to conduct a thorough vulnerability assessment, which involves systematically scanning and probing a target environment for known vulnerabilities.

Vulnerability scanning tools and techniques help ethical hackers identify and assess potential weaknesses, such as outdated software, missing patches, and misconfigured settings.

These assessments often reveal a multitude of issues that can be categorized and prioritized based on their severity and potential impact on the organization.

Once vulnerabilities are identified, ethical hackers can proceed to the exploitation phase, which involves actively testing and exploiting the weaknesses to demonstrate their impact.

Exploitation serves multiple purposes, including verifying the validity of the identified vulnerabilities, assessing their potential consequences, and providing concrete evidence to stakeholders.

Common weaknesses often include unpatched software vulnerabilities, which are vulnerabilities in software applications or operating systems that have been publicly disclosed and for which patches or updates are available.

Ethical hackers leverage these vulnerabilities to gain unauthorized access, execute malicious code, or escalate privileges within the target system.

Phishing attacks, a prevalent form of social engineering, target human weaknesses by manipulating individuals into revealing sensitive information, clicking on malicious links, or downloading infected files.

Ethical hackers may design and execute phishing campaigns to assess an organization's susceptibility to these common weaknesses.

Password-related weaknesses are pervasive in many organizations, including weak or easily guessable passwords, password reuse, and inadequate password policies.

Ethical hackers use techniques like password cracking, brute-force attacks, and dictionary attacks to test the strength of passwords and identify weak points in authentication mechanisms.

Common weaknesses also extend to network security, where misconfigured firewalls, open ports, and insecure wireless networks can expose organizations to risks.

Ethical hackers examine network configurations, conduct port scans, and assess firewall rules to identify vulnerabilities that could be exploited by attackers.

Web applications are frequent targets for ethical hacking assessments, as they often contain vulnerabilities that can be exploited to compromise sensitive data or gain unauthorized access.

Common weaknesses in web applications include SQL injection, cross-site scripting (XSS), and insecure authentication mechanisms.

Ethical hackers perform detailed assessments of web applications, probing for these vulnerabilities and demonstrating their potential impact.

Physical security weaknesses, such as lax access controls, inadequate surveillance, and poor facility design, can leave organizations vulnerable to unauthorized access and breaches.

Ethical hackers may conduct physical security assessments, including penetration testing of physical access points and social engineering tests to bypass security measures.

Common weaknesses also encompass misconfigurations in cloud environments, where organizations often struggle to properly secure their cloud-based assets and resources.

Ethical hackers examine cloud configurations, assess access controls, and identify misconfigured settings that could expose sensitive data or systems.

Additionally, insider threats, where employees or trusted individuals exploit their access to harm the organization, are considered common weaknesses.

Ethical hackers assess the organization's ability to detect and respond to insider threats by simulating insider attacks and evaluating the effectiveness of security controls.

In the process of identifying and exploiting common weaknesses, ethical hackers adhere to strict rules of engagement, ensuring that their actions are authorized, controlled, and conducted within the agreed-upon scope.

Furthermore, ethical hackers maintain transparency and clear communication with the organization, providing regular updates on their progress and findings throughout the engagement.

Upon identifying and exploiting common weaknesses, ethical hackers compile detailed reports that include a comprehensive assessment of vulnerabilities, their potential impact, and recommendations for remediation.

These reports serve as valuable resources for organizations to prioritize and address security weaknesses effectively.

In summary, identifying and exploiting common weaknesses is a fundamental aspect of ethical hacking, enabling security professionals to uncover vulnerabilities, assess their impact, and provide actionable recommendations for remediation.

By systematically testing and assessing common weaknesses across various dimensions of cybersecurity, ethical hackers help organizations strengthen their security posture and defend against potential threats and attacks.

Zero-day vulnerabilities and exploits represent a significant challenge in the world of cybersecurity, posing a threat to organizations, governments, and individuals alike.

These vulnerabilities are called "zero-day" because they are exploited by attackers on the same day they are discovered, leaving zero days for organizations to prepare and defend against them.

Zero-day vulnerabilities are flaws or weaknesses in software, hardware, or firmware that are unknown to the vendor or developer and have not been patched or fixed.

This means that there are no available security updates or patches to address these vulnerabilities, leaving systems and applications exposed to potential attacks.

Zero-day exploits, on the other hand, are malicious programs or techniques developed to take advantage of these undisclosed vulnerabilities.

Attackers use zero-day exploits to gain unauthorized access to systems, steal sensitive data, disrupt operations, or compromise security.

The covert nature of zero-day vulnerabilities and exploits makes them highly sought after by cybercriminals, state-sponsored actors, and hacking groups.

The discovery and exploitation of zero-day vulnerabilities can lead to significant financial losses, reputation damage, and national security risks.

One of the most concerning aspects of zero-day vulnerabilities is their stealthy nature.

Because they are unknown to the vendor or developer, there are typically no known defense mechanisms or security controls in place to protect against them.

This makes zero-day vulnerabilities particularly dangerous, as they can be used to breach even well-defended systems.

The process of discovering a zero-day vulnerability typically begins with a security researcher or ethical hacker conducting a thorough analysis of software, hardware, or firmware.

This analysis may involve reverse engineering, code auditing, and fuzz testing to identify potential flaws or weaknesses.

Once a zero-day vulnerability is discovered, the researcher faces an ethical dilemma.

They must decide whether to report the vulnerability to the vendor or developer for responsible disclosure or to sell it on the black market to the highest bidder, which may include cybercriminals or government agencies.

Responsible disclosure is the preferred approach, as it allows the vendor or developer to create a patch or security update to protect their users.

However, responsible disclosure can be a complex and time-consuming process, as it requires coordination between the researcher and the vendor, verification of the vulnerability, and the development of a patch.

In some cases, researchers may choose to disclose the vulnerability publicly after a reasonable amount of time has passed without a patch.

This is known as full disclosure and can put pressure on vendors to address the issue promptly.

In contrast, selling a zero-day vulnerability on the black market can be lucrative but raises ethical and legal concerns. It may also contribute to a thriving underground market for zero-day exploits, making it easier for cybercriminals and state-sponsored actors to launch attacks.

Governments and intelligence agencies have been known to purchase zero-day exploits for use in cyber espionage and cyber warfare.

The secretive nature of these transactions makes it difficult to monitor or regulate the trade in zero-day vulnerabilities.

One notable example of a zero-day exploit is Stuxnet, a computer worm that targeted supervisory control and data acquisition (SCADA) systems in Iran's nuclear facilities.

Stuxnet exploited multiple zero-day vulnerabilities to gain access to the systems and manipulate their operations.

While the origins of Stuxnet remain a subject of speculation, it is widely believed to be a state-sponsored cyberweapon.

The use of zero-day exploits in incidents like Stuxnet underscores the potential impact of these vulnerabilities on critical infrastructure and national security.

To defend against zero-day vulnerabilities and exploits, organizations must adopt a proactive and multi-layered security strategy.

This includes implementing intrusion detection systems, network monitoring, and behavioral analysis to detect suspicious activities that may indicate a zero-day attack.

Regularly updating and patching software and systems, even in the absence of known vulnerabilities, can also reduce the attack surface and mitigate the risk of exploitation.

Furthermore, organizations should educate their employees about security best practices, including safe browsing habits and email hygiene, to minimize the likelihood of falling victim to zero-day exploits delivered through phishing or social engineering.

Engaging with ethical hackers and security researchers through bug bounty programs can provide organizations with valuable insights into potential vulnerabilities and weaknesses in their systems, allowing them to proactively address these issues.

In summary, zero-day vulnerabilities and exploits represent a formidable challenge in the ever-evolving landscape of cybersecurity.

Their stealthy nature and potential for significant harm make them a top priority for organizations, governments, and security professionals.

Addressing the threat of zero-day vulnerabilities requires a combination of responsible disclosure, vigilant monitoring, proactive patching, and user education to minimize the risks and consequences of exploitation.

Chapter 4: Advanced Penetration Testing

Advanced techniques for gaining access are a critical component of the ethical hacking process, allowing security professionals to assess the security of systems, applications, and networks by simulating the actions of malicious hackers. These techniques encompass a wide range of methods and approaches that ethical hackers use to identify vulnerabilities, exploit weaknesses, and gain unauthorized access to target systems.

One of the primary goals of advanced access techniques is to evaluate the effectiveness of security controls, including authentication mechanisms, access permissions, and intrusion detection systems.

By testing these controls in a controlled and authorized manner, ethical hackers help organizations identify weaknesses and improve their overall security posture.

Password attacks are among the most common advanced access techniques, as passwords are often the first line of defense for protecting systems and accounts.

Ethical hackers may use techniques like password cracking, brute-force attacks, dictionary attacks, and rainbow table attacks to attempt to guess or recover passwords.

These attacks are used to assess the strength of passwords and identify weak or easily guessable ones.

Social engineering attacks are another category of advanced access techniques that target human weaknesses rather than technical vulnerabilities.

These attacks manipulate individuals into divulging sensitive information, clicking on malicious links, or performing actions that compromise security.

Social engineering techniques may include phishing, pretexting, baiting, tailgating, and spear phishing.

Phishing attacks, for example, involve sending deceptive emails or messages to trick recipients into revealing login credentials or other sensitive data.

Pretexting involves creating a fabricated scenario or pretext to gain access to information or systems.

Baiting attacks entice individuals with enticing offers or rewards to download malicious files or click on links.

Tailgating exploits physical security weaknesses by gaining unauthorized physical access to a restricted area by following an authorized individual.

Spear phishing is a targeted form of phishing that tailors deceptive messages to specific individuals or organizations, making them more convincing.

Advanced access techniques also include privilege escalation, which involves attempting to elevate user privileges or gain administrative access to systems.

This may include exploiting vulnerabilities in software, misconfigurations, or weak access controls to gain higher-level privileges than originally granted.

Common privilege escalation techniques include kernel exploits, privilege escalation vulnerabilities, and abusing misconfigured permissions.

Kernel exploits target vulnerabilities in the core of an operating system to gain elevated privileges, often requiring knowledge of operating system internals.

Privilege escalation vulnerabilities are flaws in software or systems that allow an attacker to escalate their privileges.

Misconfigured permissions may grant unintended access to files, directories, or services, enabling attackers to escalate their privileges.

Buffer overflow attacks are advanced access techniques used to exploit vulnerabilities in software applications, leading to unauthorized access or code execution.

These attacks occur when an attacker overflows a program's buffer, overwriting memory locations and potentially gaining control over the program's execution.

Buffer overflow attacks can lead to remote code execution, allowing attackers to execute arbitrary code on a target system.

Web application attacks are a subset of advanced access techniques focused on exploiting vulnerabilities in web applications and websites.

Common web application attacks include SQL injection, cross-site scripting (XSS), and remote file inclusion (RFI) attacks.

SQL injection attacks manipulate a web application's database queries to gain unauthorized access to the database or execute malicious code.

Cross-site scripting attacks inject malicious scripts into web pages viewed by other users, potentially stealing their session cookies or executing actions on their behalf.

RFI attacks allow attackers to include remote files on a web server, potentially executing arbitrary code or gaining unauthorized access.

Wireless network attacks are advanced techniques used to compromise wireless networks and gain unauthorized access to them.

These attacks may involve cracking Wi-Fi encryption, intercepting wireless communications, or launching deauthentication attacks to disconnect users from a network.

Ethical hackers use wireless network attacks to identify vulnerabilities in Wi-Fi networks and improve their security.

Advanced access techniques also encompass zero-day exploits, which target undisclosed vulnerabilities in software, hardware, or firmware.

Zero-day exploits take advantage of vulnerabilities that have not yet been patched by the vendor or developer, making them particularly potent.

Ethical hackers may discover and responsibly disclose zero-day vulnerabilities or use them in controlled environments to assess their potential impact.

Post-exploitation techniques are used after gaining access to a system to maintain control and further compromise the target.

These techniques may include establishing backdoors, maintaining persistence, and escalating privileges to ensure continued access.

Exploiting advanced access techniques requires careful planning, ethical considerations, and adherence to legal and authorized boundaries.

Ethical hackers must ensure that their actions are conducted within the scope of their engagements and with proper authorization from the organization being tested.

Furthermore, advanced access techniques are used to improve security by identifying vulnerabilities and weaknesses that can be addressed and mitigated.

Regularly assessing and testing systems and applications using these techniques is essential to maintaining a robust security posture.

In summary, advanced techniques for gaining access are a critical component of ethical hacking, allowing security professionals to evaluate and strengthen the security of systems, applications, and networks.

These techniques encompass a wide range of methods, including password attacks, social engineering, privilege escalation, buffer overflow attacks, web application attacks, wireless network attacks, zero-day exploits, and post-exploitation techniques.

By conducting ethical hacking assessments using advanced access techniques, organizations can proactively identify and remediate vulnerabilities, reducing the risk of unauthorized access and security breaches.

Post-exploitation and privilege escalation are critical phases in ethical hacking that occur after an attacker has successfully gained unauthorized access to a system or network.

These phases involve maintaining control over the compromised system, escalating privileges to gain deeper access, and potentially moving laterally within the environment.

The post-exploitation phase is a crucial step for attackers to achieve their objectives, whether those objectives involve data exfiltration, further compromise, or espionage.

In ethical hacking, these phases are conducted for the purpose of testing and assessing the security controls and measures in place within an organization.

During the post-exploitation phase, ethical hackers aim to simulate the actions and tactics that real attackers might employ.

One of the primary goals of post-exploitation is to establish persistence, which involves ensuring that the attacker's access to the compromised system remains even after a reboot or system updates.

Establishing persistence can be achieved through various means, including creating backdoors, scheduled tasks, and registry modifications.

Backdoors are pieces of code or software that allow an attacker to regain access to a compromised system without needing to go through the initial exploitation process again.

Scheduled tasks are scripts or processes that run at predefined times or events, and attackers can use them to maintain control over a system.

Registry modifications involve making changes to the Windows Registry or other configuration settings that grant an attacker continued access.

Maintaining persistence is essential for attackers to avoid detection and continue their activities within the compromised environment.

Privilege escalation is another critical aspect of post-exploitation, as it allows attackers to gain higher-level privileges than initially acquired.

In many cases, attackers start with limited user privileges but seek to escalate their access to gain administrative or root-level privileges.

This escalation provides them with more control over the system and access to critical resources.

Privilege escalation techniques vary depending on the operating system and application vulnerabilities that can be exploited.

Common privilege escalation methods include exploiting vulnerabilities in software, abusing misconfigured permissions, and leveraging known privilege escalation exploits.

Software vulnerabilities can be exploited to execute code with higher privileges than originally granted, effectively elevating an attacker's access.

Misconfigured permissions may grant unintended access to sensitive files, directories, or services, which can then be used for privilege escalation.

Known privilege escalation exploits target weaknesses in the operating system or software applications, enabling attackers to escalate their privileges.

Once privilege escalation is achieved, attackers can execute more advanced and malicious actions on the compromised system.

Lateral movement is another concept closely related to post-exploitation, as it involves the attacker's ability to move through the network from one compromised system to another.

Attackers seek to expand their reach within the network, compromising additional systems and potentially moving toward high-value targets.

Lateral movement techniques may include using stolen credentials, pass-the-hash attacks, and exploiting vulnerabilities in network protocols or services.

Pass-the-hash attacks involve the theft and use of hashed password data to gain access to other systems.

Stolen credentials, obtained through various means like keyloggers or brute-force attacks, can be used to authenticate and move laterally within the network.

Exploiting vulnerabilities in network protocols or services can lead to the compromise of additional systems within the environment.

Post-exploitation also includes activities related to data exfiltration, which involves stealing sensitive information from the compromised systems or network.

Attackers may use various techniques to exfiltrate data, such as uploading files to external servers, sending data through covert channels, or using encryption to hide their activities.

Ethical hackers conducting post-exploitation assessments aim to identify vulnerabilities and weaknesses in an organization's security measures that may allow attackers to establish persistence, escalate privileges, and move laterally.

By simulating these activities, ethical hackers help organizations understand their security vulnerabilities and take measures to prevent, detect, and respond to such attacks effectively.

Organizations can use the insights gained from post-exploitation assessments to enhance their security posture, implement stronger access controls, and improve their incident response capabilities.

In summary, post-exploitation and privilege escalation are crucial phases in ethical hacking, allowing security professionals to assess the effectiveness of an organization's security measures and identify vulnerabilities that could lead to unauthorized access, escalation of privileges, and data exfiltration.

By simulating these activities, ethical hackers help organizations improve their security defenses and protect against real-world threats.

Chapter 5: Web Application Security Assessment

The OWASP Top Ten Vulnerabilities is a widely recognized and influential list that highlights the most critical web application security risks faced by organizations today.

These vulnerabilities, identified by the Open Web Application Security Project (OWASP), serve as a guide for security professionals, developers, and organizations to prioritize and address common threats.

The OWASP Top Ten list is updated periodically to reflect the evolving threat landscape and emerging security risks.

Understanding and mitigating these vulnerabilities is essential for safeguarding web applications and protecting sensitive data from exploitation.

The first vulnerability on the OWASP Top Ten list is Injection, which refers to attacks that occur when untrusted data is sent to an interpreter as part of a command or query.

Injection vulnerabilities can manifest in various forms, including SQL injection, NoSQL injection, and command injection, and they allow attackers to manipulate the behavior of the interpreter.

The second vulnerability is Broken Authentication, which occurs when authentication and session management mechanisms are flawed or improperly implemented.

Attackers can exploit these weaknesses to gain unauthorized access to user accounts, impersonate legitimate users, or perform actions on behalf of others.

Sensitive data exposure is the third vulnerability, involving the exposure of sensitive information, such as passwords or credit card numbers, due to inadequate security controls.

This exposure can result from poor encryption, weak authentication, or insufficient access controls.

XML External Entities (XXE) is the fourth vulnerability on the list, and it involves the improper handling of XML data that may contain external entity references.

XXE attacks can lead to data disclosure, denial of service, or remote code execution.

Security Misconfiguration is the fifth vulnerability and arises from improperly configured security settings or weak default configurations.

Attackers can exploit these misconfigurations to access sensitive data or execute unauthorized actions.

The sixth vulnerability is Cross-Site Scripting (XSS), a common web application flaw that allows attackers to inject malicious scripts into web pages viewed by other users.

XSS attacks can steal session cookies, redirect users to malicious websites, or perform actions on behalf of the victim.

Insecure Deserialization is the seventh vulnerability, which occurs when an application improperly processes serialized data, leading to remote code execution or other security issues.

Using components with known vulnerabilities is the eighth vulnerability, as it exposes applications to exploits that target outdated or insecure software libraries or components.

The ninth vulnerability is insufficient logging and monitoring, which hinders an organization's ability to detect and respond to security incidents effectively.

Without adequate logging and monitoring, attackers can carry out malicious activities without detection.

The final vulnerability on the OWASP Top Ten list is Broken Access Control, which occurs when users can access unauthorized functionality or data by manipulating URLs, form fields, or other parameters.

Attackers can exploit this weakness to gain elevated privileges, view sensitive data, or perform actions beyond their intended permissions.

Addressing the OWASP Top Ten vulnerabilities requires a multifaceted approach that involves secure coding practices, thorough testing, and ongoing monitoring.

Developers should follow secure coding guidelines, validate and sanitize input data, implement proper authentication and session management, and use encryption to protect sensitive information.

Security testing, including automated and manual assessments, should be conducted throughout the development lifecycle to identify and remediate vulnerabilities.

Regular vulnerability scanning, penetration testing, and code reviews help organizations uncover and address security flaws.

Effective logging and monitoring systems enable organizations to detect and respond to suspicious activities promptly.

Additionally, keeping software and components up to date and patching known vulnerabilities is essential to mitigate risks associated with vulnerable software libraries.

By prioritizing the mitigation of OWASP Top Ten vulnerabilities, organizations can enhance the security of their web applications and reduce the risk of data breaches, unauthorized access, and other security incidents.

Ultimately, addressing these vulnerabilities contributes to a more resilient and secure digital landscape for businesses and users alike.

Automated and manual testing approaches are two essential methodologies employed in software quality assurance and testing to ensure that applications and systems meet their intended objectives while maintaining security and functionality.

Automated testing involves the use of specialized software tools and scripts to execute test cases, validate functionality, and identify defects or vulnerabilities in an application.

This approach is efficient for repetitive and regression testing, where tests need to be repeatedly executed with different inputs or configurations.

Automated testing is particularly valuable in scenarios where a large number of test cases must be executed quickly, such as during the development of complex software applications.

The primary advantage of automated testing is its ability to save time and effort, as once test scripts are developed, they can be run repeatedly without human intervention.

Furthermore, automated testing can provide detailed reports and logs, making it easier to identify and reproduce issues, which in turn speeds up the debugging and resolution process.

However, automated testing is not without limitations; it is less effective for tests that require human judgment, creativity, or the evaluation of user experience.

Certain aspects of testing, such as usability, user interface design, and exploratory testing, are better suited for manual testing approaches.

Manual testing, on the other hand, relies on human testers to execute test cases, observe the application's behavior, and report defects or vulnerabilities.

Manual testing is crucial for evaluating the user experience, usability, and overall quality of an application, as it allows testers to mimic real user interactions and identify issues that automated tests might overlook.

Testers can explore different scenarios, provide subjective feedback, and assess how the application responds to unique and unexpected inputs.

This approach is particularly valuable for user interface testing, acceptance testing, and usability testing, where the emphasis is on the user's perspective and interaction with the application.

Manual testing also excels in exploratory testing, where testers explore the application to uncover defects or vulnerabilities that may not have been previously considered.

The collaboration between automated and manual testing approaches is often referred to as "manual testing with automation support" or "augmented testing."

In augmented testing, automated tests are used to handle repetitive and time-consuming tasks, such as regression testing, while manual testers focus on critical areas requiring human judgment and creativity.

This combination leverages the strengths of both approaches and ensures comprehensive test coverage.

For example, during the initial phases of development, manual testers can perform exploratory testing to uncover unexpected issues, while automated tests can continuously verify the application's core functionality.

In agile development environments, where frequent changes are made to the software, automation is crucial for maintaining efficient testing processes, while manual testing provides assurance that the application meets user expectations and requirements.

To effectively integrate automated and manual testing approaches, organizations should establish clear test objectives, determine which areas are best suited for each approach, and allocate resources accordingly.

Furthermore, test automation frameworks and tools should be chosen based on the specific needs of the project, considering factors such as the application's architecture, technology stack, and development cycle.

It's essential to strike a balance between the two approaches, recognizing that while automated testing improves efficiency, manual testing remains indispensable for evaluating the user experience and uncovering complex issues.

Moreover, the collaboration between automated and manual testers should foster communication and knowledge sharing, ensuring that both teams work cohesively towards the project's goals.

Testers should document test cases, test results, and defects in a centralized test management system, facilitating traceability and collaboration between teams.

In summary, automated and manual testing approaches each offer unique advantages and are best suited for different aspects of software testing.

Automated testing excels in efficiency, repeatability, and coverage of repetitive tasks, while manual testing is essential for evaluating user experience, usability, and exploratory testing.

The integration of both approaches, often referred to as augmented testing, enables organizations to achieve comprehensive test coverage and deliver high-quality software that meets user expectations and security standards.

By understanding the strengths and limitations of automated and manual testing, organizations can develop effective testing strategies that enhance software quality and reduce the risk of defects and vulnerabilities.

Chapter 6: Wireless Network Penetration

Cracking WEP and WPA/WPA2 encryption are activities that involve attempting to decipher the security mechanisms protecting wireless networks, with the intention of unauthorized access.

WEP (Wired Equivalent Privacy) was one of the earliest encryption protocols used to secure wireless networks.

However, it has since been widely recognized as insecure and vulnerable to various attacks.

Cracking WEP encryption often involves exploiting vulnerabilities in its encryption algorithm and key management.

One common method used to crack WEP encryption is the "ARP Request Replay" attack, where an attacker captures and replays ARP (Address Resolution Protocol) packets to gather initialization vectors (IVs) and deduce the encryption key.

Another technique, known as the "Chop-Chop Attack," involves manipulating encrypted packets and using statistical analysis to recover the key.

Furthermore, tools like Aircrack-ng are commonly used to automate the process of collecting IVs and attempting to crack WEP keys.

WEP encryption can be cracked relatively quickly, sometimes within minutes or hours, depending on the volume of captured data and the processing power of the attacker's system.

Due to its inherent weaknesses, WEP encryption is no longer considered secure and is not recommended for protecting wireless networks.

In contrast, WPA (Wi-Fi Protected Access) and WPA2 were introduced to address the vulnerabilities of WEP and provide stronger security for wireless networks.

WPA uses the Temporal Key Integrity Protocol (TKIP) for encryption, while WPA2 uses the more secure Advanced Encryption Standard (AES) protocol.

Cracking WPA/WPA2 encryption is significantly more challenging than cracking WEP, as these protocols are designed to resist various types of attacks.

One common attack against WPA/WPA2 is the "brute-force" attack, where an attacker attempts to guess the passphrase by trying various combinations until the correct one is found.

However, this approach is time-consuming and computationally intensive, making it less practical for long and complex passphrases.

Another attack is the "dictionary attack," where an attacker uses a precompiled list of common words and phrases to guess the passphrase.

While this method can be more efficient than brute-force, it relies on the likelihood that the passphrase is contained within the dictionary.

To protect against dictionary attacks, users are encouraged to use strong, unique passphrases that are not easily guessable.

Rainbow tables are also used in cracking WPA/WPA2 encryption, where precomputed tables of possible passphrases are compared to the hashed passphrase.

However, using a strong, unique passphrase can mitigate the effectiveness of rainbow table attacks.

A more advanced attack against WPA/WPA2 encryption is the "handshake capture" attack.

When a device connects to a WPA/WPA2-protected network, a four-way handshake process occurs during which the encryption keys are exchanged.

An attacker can capture this handshake and attempt to crack it offline by trying different passphrases.

Tools like Hashcat and John the Ripper can be used for this purpose, but the success of the attack depends on the complexity of the passphrase.

Cracking WPA/WPA2 encryption is significantly more challenging than WEP, and it can take days, weeks, or even longer to successfully crack a strong passphrase.

Moreover, the use of a strong, unique passphrase is crucial for protecting against these types of attacks.

To defend against unauthorized access to wireless networks, it is essential to use the latest security protocols, such as WPA3, which offers even stronger security measures and is designed to withstand modern cracking techniques.

Additionally, it is important to regularly update network equipment, install security patches, and implement strong authentication methods, such as WPA3-Enterprise, which utilizes 802.1X/EAP for network access control.

In summary, cracking WEP and WPA/WPA2 encryption involves attempts to exploit vulnerabilities in wireless network security mechanisms.

While WEP is known to be highly insecure and relatively easy to crack, WPA/WPA2 encryption provides stronger protection but is still susceptible to various attacks if weak or common passphrases are used.

To secure wireless networks effectively, users and organizations should employ the latest security protocols, use strong passphrases, and stay informed about emerging threats and vulnerabilities.

Wireless Man-in-the-Middle (MitM) attacks are a category of cybersecurity threats that occur in wireless communication environments, where an attacker intercepts and possibly alters the communication between two parties without their knowledge or consent.

These attacks are particularly concerning as they can lead to the unauthorized access of sensitive data, eavesdropping on conversations, and even the injection of malicious content into the communication stream.

Wireless networks, such as Wi-Fi, Bluetooth, and cellular networks, are susceptible to MitM attacks due to their inherent characteristics, including radio frequency communication and the broadcast nature of wireless signals.

One common method of wireless MitM attacks involves an attacker positioning themselves between the target device and the network or other communication endpoint.

This positioning allows the attacker to intercept and potentially modify the data being exchanged between the two parties.

In Wi-Fi networks, for example, attackers can create rogue access points with names similar to legitimate networks, enticing users to connect to them unwittingly.

Once connected, the attacker can intercept data packets flowing between the user's device and the rogue access point, effectively becoming a man-in-the-middle.

In Bluetooth communications, attackers can exploit vulnerabilities in pairing processes or weak encryption to intercept data exchanged between paired devices.

Cellular networks are not immune to MitM attacks either; attackers can use tools and techniques to intercept cellular signals and eavesdrop on conversations or capture data traffic.

One common scenario for wireless MitM attacks involves eavesdropping on unencrypted or weakly encrypted Wi-Fi communications.

When users connect to public Wi-Fi hotspots that lack proper security measures, attackers within proximity can intercept and monitor the data being transmitted between the user's device and the hotspot.

This interception can reveal sensitive information such as login credentials, personal messages, or financial data.

To conduct MitM attacks effectively, attackers often employ various tools and techniques, including packet sniffing software, wireless network spoofing, and malicious code injection.

Packet sniffing software, such as Wireshark, allows attackers to capture and analyze network traffic, enabling them to identify valuable data and vulnerabilities.

Wireless network spoofing involves creating fake access points that mimic legitimate networks, tricking users into connecting to them.

Once connected, all data transmitted through the rogue access point can be intercepted and monitored by the attacker.

Malicious code injection is another technique used in MitM attacks, where attackers inject malicious scripts or code into web pages or applications, leading to unintended actions or data leakage when users interact with the compromised content.

To protect against wireless MitM attacks, various security measures and best practices are essential.

The use of encryption protocols, such as WPA3 for Wi-Fi networks, helps secure data in transit, making it difficult for attackers to intercept and decipher communications.

In addition, users should be cautious when connecting to public Wi-Fi hotspots and verify the legitimacy of the network they are connecting to.

Using virtual private networks (VPNs) when connecting to untrusted networks can add an extra layer of security by encrypting data traffic between the user's device and a trusted server.

Bluetooth users should keep their devices and firmware updated to patch known vulnerabilities, and they should avoid pairing with unknown or unverified devices.

Regularly monitoring and auditing wireless networks for unauthorized or suspicious devices and activity can help organizations detect and mitigate MitM attacks.

Furthermore, implementing strong authentication methods and two-factor authentication (2FA) for accessing sensitive accounts and services can significantly reduce the risk of MitM attacks.

In enterprise environments, network segmentation, intrusion detection systems, and intrusion prevention systems can provide additional layers of security against MitM threats.

Educating users about the risks of MitM attacks and promoting safe wireless practices, such as avoiding public Wi-Fi for sensitive transactions or using secure messaging apps, can also contribute to overall cybersecurity awareness and resilience.

MitM attacks in wireless environments are a persistent threat that exploits the vulnerabilities inherent in wireless communication technologies.

By understanding the techniques and methods employed by attackers and implementing robust security measures and user education, individuals and organizations can better defend against these malicious activities and safeguard their data and privacy.

Chapter 7: Cloud Infrastructure Auditing

Auditing cloud service providers (CSPs) is a critical component of modern cybersecurity and risk management, as organizations increasingly rely on cloud computing to store, process, and manage their data and applications.

Cloud service providers offer a range of services, including Infrastructure as a Service (IaaS), Platform as a Service (PaaS), and Software as a Service (SaaS), each with its own set of security considerations.

The audit process for CSPs involves evaluating the security controls and practices they have in place to protect customer data and ensure the availability and integrity of cloud services.

One of the primary goals of auditing CSPs is to assess their compliance with security standards and regulatory requirements, such as the General Data Protection Regulation (GDPR), the Health Insurance Portability and Accountability Act (HIPAA), and the Payment Card Industry Data Security Standard (PCI DSS).

Auditors examine the CSP's policies, procedures, and technical measures to determine if they align with these standards and regulations.

Cloud service providers typically undergo third-party audits and assessments to demonstrate their compliance with industry and regulatory standards.

These audits may result in the issuance of certifications, such as SOC 2 (Service Organization Control 2) reports, which provide assurances to customers that the CSP has implemented effective security controls.

The audit process for CSPs encompasses various aspects of security, including data protection, access controls, network security, and incident response.

Data protection is a fundamental concern in the cloud, as customers entrust CSPs with their sensitive and valuable data.

Auditors evaluate how CSPs encrypt data both at rest and in transit, as well as their mechanisms for data backup, recovery, and retention.

Access controls are essential to prevent unauthorized access to cloud resources.

Auditors assess the CSP's identity and access management (IAM) practices, including user provisioning, authentication, authorization, and role-based access control.

Network security plays a crucial role in protecting cloud services from external threats.

Auditors examine the CSP's network architecture, firewall configurations, intrusion detection and prevention systems, and security monitoring capabilities.

Incident response is another critical area of evaluation, as CSPs must have procedures in place to detect, respond to, and mitigate security incidents.

Auditors assess the CSP's incident response plan, incident reporting mechanisms, and the effectiveness of their incident response team.

In addition to evaluating security controls, auditors also examine the physical security of CSP data centers, as physical access to infrastructure can pose a significant risk.

Physical security assessments include reviewing security camera footage, access logs, and visitor logs to ensure that only authorized personnel have access to data center facilities.

Auditors also evaluate the environmental controls in data centers, such as temperature and humidity monitoring, to ensure the optimal operation of hardware.

Furthermore, auditing CSPs involves assessing their business continuity and disaster recovery plans.

Organizations rely on cloud services for critical business operations, so CSPs must have plans in place to ensure service availability in the event of disruptions.

Auditors review these plans and assess their adequacy in mitigating risks and minimizing service downtime.

Another critical aspect of auditing CSPs is assessing their transparency and communication with customers.

CSPs should provide customers with clear and comprehensive information about their security practices, compliance certifications, and incident response procedures.

Auditors evaluate the CSP's transparency efforts to ensure that customers can make informed decisions regarding the security of their data in the cloud.

In addition to audits conducted by third-party organizations, organizations that use cloud services should perform their own due diligence when selecting a CSP.

This includes reviewing the CSP's security documentation, conducting security assessments, and assessing the CSP's ability to meet their specific security and compliance requirements.

While audits and assessments provide valuable insights into the security practices of CSPs, organizations should also consider contractual agreements and service level agreements (SLAs) to define the security responsibilities of both parties.

These agreements should clearly outline the security controls, responsibilities, and obligations of the CSP and the customer.

Regularly reviewing and updating these agreements is essential to ensure that they reflect the evolving security landscape and the specific needs of the organization.

In summary, auditing cloud service providers is a critical aspect of cybersecurity and risk management in the modern digital landscape.

It involves assessing the security controls, compliance, transparency, and business continuity measures of CSPs to ensure the protection of customer data and the availability of cloud services.

Audits and assessments, both by third-party organizations and by the customer, play a vital role in evaluating the security posture of CSPs and making informed decisions about cloud adoption.

By conducting thorough audits and maintaining clear contractual agreements, organizations can navigate the complexities of cloud security and leverage the benefits of cloud computing while mitigating risks effectively.

Ensuring data privacy and security in the cloud is a paramount concern for organizations and individuals alike in today's interconnected digital world.

The adoption of cloud computing has brought about numerous benefits, including cost-efficiency, scalability, and accessibility, but it has also introduced unique challenges and risks related to the protection of sensitive information.

Data privacy and security are fundamental aspects of maintaining trust and compliance in cloud environments.

One of the key principles in safeguarding data in the cloud is encryption, which involves the transformation of data into a secure, unreadable format that can only be decrypted by authorized parties.

Encryption helps protect data both at rest and in transit, ensuring that even if unauthorized access occurs, the data remains inaccessible to malicious actors.

Data encryption should be applied consistently across all cloud services and storage solutions used by an organization to maintain a strong security posture.

However, encryption is just one part of the equation; effective key management is equally critical.

Organizations must implement robust key management practices to securely generate, store, and rotate encryption keys.

Access control is another vital element in safeguarding data in the cloud.

Access controls define who can access specific resources and what actions they can perform.

Implementing strong identity and access management (IAM) practices ensures that only authorized users and services can access sensitive data.

IAM solutions provide mechanisms for user authentication, authorization, and access control policies, allowing organizations to enforce the principle of least privilege.

Multi-factor authentication (MFA) further enhances security by requiring users to provide multiple forms of verification before granting access.

To maintain data privacy and security, organizations should regularly review and audit access control policies to ensure they align with their security requirements.

Data classification is an essential practice in the cloud, helping organizations identify and label sensitive data based on its level of confidentiality.

Classifying data allows organizations to apply appropriate security controls and encryption based on the data's sensitivity.

Additionally, data classification aids in compliance efforts by enabling organizations to meet regulatory requirements related to data handling and protection.

Cloud providers offer various tools and services for data classification, including automated tagging and classification based on predefined policies.

Compliance with regulatory frameworks and industry standards is a crucial aspect of data privacy and security in the cloud.

Different industries and regions have specific data protection and privacy regulations that organizations must adhere to.

For instance, the General Data Protection Regulation (GDPR) in the European Union and the Health Insurance Portability and Accountability Act (HIPAA) in the United States impose strict requirements on the handling and protection of personal and healthcare data, respectively.

Organizations must ensure that their cloud deployments comply with these regulations by implementing appropriate controls, conducting regular audits, and maintaining documentation to demonstrate compliance.

Security monitoring and incident response capabilities are essential components of a cloud security strategy.

Proactive monitoring of cloud resources and network traffic allows organizations to detect suspicious activities and potential security breaches.

Real-time alerts and automated responses enable rapid incident detection and mitigation.

Incident response plans should be well-defined and tested to ensure an efficient and coordinated response to security incidents.

Cloud providers offer a range of security monitoring tools and services that organizations can leverage to enhance their security posture.

Furthermore, organizations should conduct regular vulnerability assessments and penetration testing on their cloud environments to identify and remediate security weaknesses before they can be exploited by attackers.

Patch management is crucial to address security vulnerabilities promptly.

Cloud providers release regular updates and patches to their services, and organizations must stay current with these updates to mitigate known security risks.

DevSecOps practices, which integrate security into the software development and deployment lifecycle, can help organizations maintain a secure and compliant cloud environment.

Educating employees and users about security best practices and potential threats is a vital aspect of data privacy and security.

Phishing attacks, social engineering, and insider threats can compromise cloud security, so organizations should provide training and awareness programs to promote a security-conscious culture.

Data backups and disaster recovery plans are essential for ensuring data availability and business continuity in the cloud.

Organizations should regularly back up critical data and test their disaster recovery plans to ensure they can quickly recover from data loss or system outages.

Maintaining an audit trail of all actions and events in the cloud environment is necessary for compliance and forensic purposes.

Cloud providers often offer comprehensive logging and monitoring services, enabling organizations to track user activities and system events.

Additionally, organizations should establish clear incident response procedures to investigate security incidents thoroughly and take appropriate actions.

In summary, ensuring data privacy and security in the cloud requires a holistic and proactive approach that encompasses encryption, access controls, data classification, compliance, security monitoring, incident response, vulnerability management, patch management, and user education.

By implementing robust security measures and best practices, organizations can mitigate risks and safeguard their data and operations in the cloud, thereby capitalizing on the benefits of cloud computing while maintaining the trust of their stakeholders and customers.

Chapter 8: Insider Threat Mitigation

Identifying insider threat indicators is a critical aspect of cybersecurity and risk management, as insider threats pose a significant risk to organizations' data, intellectual property, and sensitive information.

Insider threats are malicious or unintentional actions taken by individuals within an organization who have access to sensitive data or systems and use that access to compromise security.

These threats can come from employees, contractors, or business partners who may have legitimate access to an organization's resources.

One of the primary challenges in identifying insider threat indicators is that insiders often have legitimate access to the systems and data they target.

This makes it challenging to distinguish between normal, authorized activities and suspicious or malicious actions.

However, there are common indicators and behavioral patterns that organizations can monitor to detect potential insider threats.

Anomalous or unusual behavior is a significant insider threat indicator.

This can include employees accessing systems or data that are not relevant to their job responsibilities, particularly if this access occurs outside of their normal working hours or from unusual locations.

Another indicator is a sudden increase in data access or data transfer activities, especially when it involves sensitive or confidential information.

For example, an employee who typically accesses a small amount of data suddenly downloading a large volume of sensitive files may raise suspicion.

Changes in an employee's behavior or work patterns can also be indicative of an insider threat.

This includes sudden changes in job performance, increased use of personal devices for work-related tasks, or a decline in job satisfaction or engagement.

Monitoring for changes in communication patterns can also provide insights into insider threats.

An employee who starts communicating with unauthorized individuals, sharing confidential information, or engaging in suspicious online discussions may be a cause for concern.

Access to privileged or restricted areas or systems without a legitimate reason can be a clear indicator of insider threats.

Unauthorized access to sensitive areas or systems can occur physically or virtually, and organizations should monitor both types of access.

Security incidents such as data breaches, unauthorized data disclosures, or system compromises should be investigated thoroughly as they may be the result of insider threats.

For example, if an organization experiences a breach that exposes sensitive data, it is essential to determine if an insider played a role in the incident.

Changes in an employee's financial situation can also be a potential insider threat indicator.

In some cases, individuals facing financial difficulties may be more susceptible to insider threats, such as theft of intellectual property or selling sensitive information.

Insider threats can also manifest in the form of malicious actions, such as intentionally introducing malware, backdoors, or other vulnerabilities into an organization's systems.

Monitoring for unauthorized software installations or changes to system configurations can help detect these insider threats.

It's important to note that insider threats can be both intentional and unintentional.

Unintentional insider threats occur when employees or individuals inadvertently cause security incidents due to negligence or lack of awareness.

For example, an employee may accidentally send sensitive information to the wrong recipient or fall victim to a phishing attack, leading to a security breach.

To effectively identify insider threat indicators, organizations should implement a robust insider threat detection program.

This program should include a combination of technical controls, behavioral analysis, and employee training.

Technical controls can include monitoring and logging of user activities, network traffic analysis, and the use of data loss prevention (DLP) solutions to identify and prevent unauthorized data transfers.

Behavioral analysis involves continuously monitoring employee activities and comparing them to established baselines to identify anomalies and potential threats.

Employee training is essential for creating awareness and promoting a culture of security within the organization.

Training should cover topics such as recognizing phishing attempts, reporting suspicious activities, and adhering to security policies and procedures.

Insider threat detection programs should also establish clear incident response procedures to investigate and mitigate insider threats promptly.

These procedures should involve collaboration between IT, security, human resources, and legal teams to ensure a comprehensive response.

In summary, identifying insider threat indicators is a crucial aspect of cybersecurity, as insider threats can pose significant risks to organizations' data and operations.

Insider threats can take various forms, both intentional and unintentional, making it challenging to detect them.

However, by monitoring for anomalous behavior, unauthorized access, changes in communication patterns, and other indicators, organizations can enhance their ability to identify and mitigate insider threats effectively.

Implementing a robust insider threat detection program that combines technical controls, behavioral analysis, and employee training is essential for safeguarding against insider threats and maintaining a secure and resilient cybersecurity posture. Implementing insider threat prevention measures is a critical aspect of cybersecurity and risk management for organizations aiming to protect their sensitive data and intellectual property from potential internal threats. Insider threats, whether intentional or unintentional, can have a significant impact on an organization's security and reputation.

To effectively prevent insider threats, organizations should adopt a multifaceted approach that encompasses technology, policies, procedures, and employee awareness.

One of the foundational elements of insider threat prevention is the development and enforcement of clear security policies and procedures.

These policies should define acceptable use of company resources, data handling procedures, access control requirements, and incident reporting protocols.

Employees should receive training on these policies and understand the consequences of violating them.

Access control is a crucial component of insider threat prevention.

Organizations should implement robust access control mechanisms to ensure that employees only have access to the systems and data necessary for their job roles.

This includes the principle of least privilege, which restricts access to the minimum level required for an employee to perform their duties effectively.

Access control should also encompass strong authentication methods, such as multi-factor authentication (MFA), to enhance security.

Data encryption is essential for protecting sensitive information from insider threats.

Data at rest and in transit should be encrypted to prevent unauthorized access, even if an insider gains access to the data.

Encryption keys should be adequately managed to ensure their security.

Monitoring user activities and network traffic is a critical aspect of insider threat prevention.

Organizations should deploy security information and event management (SIEM) systems and intrusion detection systems (IDS) to detect suspicious activities or anomalies.

Real-time monitoring and automated alerts can help organizations respond quickly to potential insider threats.

User and entity behavior analytics (UEBA) can aid in identifying abnormal behaviors and patterns that may indicate insider threats.

Monitoring should also extend to privileged users and administrators who have access to sensitive systems and data.

Implementing strong user authentication measures, including privileged access management (PAM), can help control and monitor privileged account usage.

Insider threat prevention should involve regular auditing and vulnerability assessments of the organization's systems and infrastructure.

These assessments can identify weaknesses that insiders might exploit and enable organizations to remediate vulnerabilities proactively.

Regularly updating and patching software and systems is crucial to prevent insider threats from exploiting known vulnerabilities.

Social engineering attacks, such as phishing, are a common vector for insider threats.

Organizations should provide security awareness training to employees to help them recognize and resist social engineering attempts.

Training should cover topics like phishing awareness, secure password practices, and safe internet browsing habits.

Whistleblower programs and anonymous reporting channels can encourage employees to report suspicious activities or concerns without fear of retaliation.

These programs can help organizations detect and address insider threats early.

Human resources policies should also be aligned with insider threat prevention efforts.

Organizations should conduct thorough background checks and reference checks when hiring new employees, particularly those who will have access to sensitive information.

Exit procedures should involve revoking access privileges and conducting exit interviews to ensure the return of company-owned assets.

Implementing data loss prevention (DLP) solutions can help prevent insider threats from unintentionally or maliciously sharing sensitive data outside the organization.

DLP solutions can monitor and control the movement of data, preventing unauthorized transfers.

Endpoint security solutions should be employed to protect individual devices and endpoints from insider threats.

This includes antivirus software, endpoint detection and response (EDR) solutions, and mobile device management (MDM) for mobile devices.

Implementing secure email gateways can help prevent phishing attacks and email-based insider threats.

These gateways can scan email content for malicious attachments or links and block or quarantine suspicious messages.

Insider threat prevention efforts should be incorporated into the organization's incident response plan.

The plan should outline procedures for investigating and responding to suspected insider threats, including legal and human resources involvement.

Regularly reviewing and updating insider threat prevention measures is essential as the threat landscape evolves.

Organizations should adapt their strategies to address emerging threats and vulnerabilities.

In summary, implementing insider threat prevention measures is a critical component of cybersecurity for organizations seeking to protect their sensitive data and intellectual property.

Insider threats, whether intentional or unintentional, pose a significant risk, and a multifaceted approach is required to mitigate these risks effectively.

This approach includes security policies, access control, encryption, monitoring, user awareness, auditing, social engineering resistance, whistleblower programs, HR policies, data loss prevention, endpoint security, email security, and incident response planning.

By proactively addressing insider threats, organizations can strengthen their security posture and safeguard their data and operations against potential internal threats.

Chapter 9: Security Compliance and Standards

An overview of security frameworks is essential for organizations striving to establish robust cybersecurity practices and protect their information assets.

Security frameworks provide structured guidelines, best practices, and standards to help organizations assess, plan, and implement effective security measures.

One widely recognized security framework is the International Organization for Standardization (ISO) 27001.

ISO 27001 is a global standard that outlines the requirements for establishing, implementing, maintaining, and continually improving an information security management system (ISMS).

Organizations that adhere to ISO 27001 can systematically manage information security risks and demonstrate their commitment to protecting sensitive data.

The National Institute of Standards and Technology (NIST) offers another prominent security framework, specifically the NIST Cybersecurity Framework.

The NIST Cybersecurity Framework provides a flexible approach for organizations to manage and reduce cybersecurity risk.

It consists of five core functions: Identify, Protect, Detect, Respond, and Recover, which help organizations prioritize and manage security efforts effectively.

The NIST Cybersecurity Framework is widely adopted in the United States and has gained recognition globally.

Another noteworthy framework is the Center for Internet Security (CIS) Critical Security Controls, also known as the CIS Controls.

The CIS Controls are a set of best practices that organizations can implement to enhance their cybersecurity posture.

These controls focus on foundational security measures that are effective at mitigating common cyber threats.

The CIS Controls are organized into three implementation groups based on an organization's size, complexity, and resources.

The Payment Card Industry Data Security Standard (PCI DSS) is a security framework specifically designed for organizations that handle payment card data.

PCI DSS outlines a set of security requirements and best practices to protect cardholder data and ensure secure payment card transactions.

Organizations that process payment card transactions are required to comply with PCI DSS to safeguard sensitive financial information.

The CIS Controls are organized into three implementation groups based on an organization's size, complexity, and resources.

The Payment Card Industry Data Security Standard (PCI DSS) is a security framework specifically designed for organizations that handle payment card data.

PCI DSS outlines a set of security requirements and best practices to protect cardholder data and ensure secure payment card transactions.

Organizations that process payment card transactions are required to comply with PCI DSS to safeguard sensitive financial information.

The Federal Risk and Authorization Management Program (FedRAMP) is a U.S. government program that standardizes the security assessment, authorization, and continuous monitoring processes for cloud products and services.

FedRAMP ensures that cloud service providers meet stringent security requirements before they can offer their services to federal agencies.

The Health Insurance Portability and Accountability Act (HIPAA) Security Rule is a framework designed to protect the confidentiality, integrity, and availability of electronic protected health information (ePHI) in the healthcare industry.

HIPAA requires covered entities and business associates to implement safeguards and controls to protect patient data.

The European Union's General Data Protection Regulation (GDPR) is a regulatory framework that governs the protection of personal data of EU residents.

GDPR imposes strict requirements on organizations that process personal data, including data protection impact assessments, data breach notifications, and the appointment of data protection officers.

The Center for Internet Security (CIS) Critical Security Controls, the Payment Card Industry Data Security Standard (PCI DSS), the Federal Risk and Authorization Management Program (FedRAMP), the Health Insurance Portability and Accountability Act (HIPAA) Security Rule, and the General Data Protection Regulation (GDPR) are just a few examples of security frameworks that organizations may need to consider based on their industry and regulatory requirements.

Each of these frameworks provides a structured approach to addressing specific security concerns and compliance obligations.

Organizations should carefully evaluate their unique needs and objectives when selecting and implementing security frameworks.

Additionally, some organizations may choose to adopt a combination of multiple frameworks to create a comprehensive security program tailored to their specific circumstances.

Ultimately, the adoption of security frameworks is a strategic decision that should align with an organization's risk management goals and regulatory obligations.

While these frameworks provide valuable guidance, organizations must also tailor their security programs to address their unique operational and technological environments.

Regular assessments, audits, and updates to security measures are essential to ensure ongoing compliance and effectiveness in mitigating evolving cyber threats.

In summary, an overview of security frameworks highlights the importance of structured guidance and best practices for organizations seeking to enhance their cybersecurity posture.

Frameworks like ISO 27001, NIST Cybersecurity Framework, CIS Critical Security Controls, PCI DSS, FedRAMP, HIPAA Security Rule, and GDPR provide valuable resources for organizations to assess and improve their security practices.

Choosing the appropriate framework or combination of frameworks depends on an organization's industry, regulatory requirements, and specific security needs.

Ultimately, a well-implemented security framework can serve as a foundation for a robust and proactive cybersecurity program that effectively protects an organization's information assets.

Achieving compliance and auditing standards is a critical endeavor for organizations operating in various industries and sectors.

Compliance refers to the adherence to specific rules, regulations, laws, and standards that are applicable to an organization's operations.

These regulations are often put in place to protect sensitive information, maintain consumer trust, ensure fair business practices, and enhance cybersecurity.

Auditing, on the other hand, is the process of systematically reviewing an organization's processes, practices, and controls to ensure they align with established standards and compliance requirements.

Achieving compliance and auditing standards involves a series of steps, strategies, and considerations that organizations must address to meet their legal and regulatory obligations.

One of the fundamental steps in achieving compliance is identifying and understanding the relevant regulations and standards that apply to the organization's operations.

This may include industry-specific regulations, regional or national laws, and international standards such as ISO (International Organization for Standardization) and NIST (National Institute of Standards and Technology).

Once the applicable regulations and standards are identified, organizations need to assess their current state of compliance.

This involves conducting a gap analysis to determine where the organization currently stands in relation to the requirements of the regulations and standards.

Gap analysis helps organizations identify areas that need improvement and serves as the foundation for developing a compliance and auditing strategy.

Developing a compliance and auditing strategy involves establishing clear objectives, goals, and a roadmap for achieving and maintaining compliance.

This strategy should outline the specific steps, resources, and timelines required to address compliance gaps and ensure ongoing adherence to regulations and standards.

A critical component of achieving compliance is creating and implementing robust policies and procedures.

These documents serve as the framework for how the organization will operate in accordance with regulatory requirements.

Policies and procedures should cover areas such as data protection, privacy, security, financial controls, and ethical conduct.

To effectively implement policies and procedures, organizations must communicate these guidelines to employees and provide training to ensure understanding and compliance.

It is essential to designate individuals or teams responsible for overseeing compliance efforts and conducting regular audits and assessments.

These compliance officers or teams play a crucial role in monitoring the organization's adherence to regulations and standards and addressing any identified issues promptly.

Compliance management software and tools can be valuable assets for tracking and managing compliance activities, including audits, assessments, and documentation.

Organizations should also establish a mechanism for reporting and addressing compliance violations or breaches.

This reporting structure should encourage employees to come forward with concerns and ensure that violations are addressed in a timely and appropriate manner.

Conducting regular internal audits is a proactive measure to assess and verify compliance with regulations and standards.

Internal audits involve reviewing the organization's processes, controls, and documentation to identify non-compliance issues and areas for improvement.

Auditors should use established criteria and checklists to guide their assessments and provide recommendations for corrective actions.

In addition to internal audits, organizations may be subject to external audits conducted by regulatory bodies, industry associations, or third-party assessors.

External audits are typically more formal and require organizations to demonstrate their adherence to specific regulations and standards.

Preparing for external audits involves thorough documentation, evidence collection, and cooperation with auditors to ensure a smooth audit process.

Achieving compliance and auditing standards is an ongoing effort that requires continuous monitoring and improvement.

Organizations should regularly review and update their compliance strategies, policies, and procedures to adapt to evolving regulatory requirements and industry best practices.

Furthermore, organizations should stay informed about changes in regulations and standards that may impact their operations and adjust their compliance efforts accordingly.

Collaboration with industry peers and participation in relevant associations and forums can provide valuable insights and guidance on compliance trends and challenges.

Ultimately, achieving compliance and auditing standards is not just a matter of meeting legal requirements but also a means of building trust with customers, partners, and stakeholders.

Organizations that prioritize compliance and adhere to high standards of ethical conduct are better positioned to thrive in today's complex and regulated business environment.

In summary, achieving compliance and auditing standards is a multifaceted process that involves identifying relevant regulations and standards, conducting gap analyses, developing a compliance strategy, creating policies and procedures, assigning responsibilities, training employees, implementing monitoring tools, and conducting regular audits.

Compliance is an ongoing effort that requires adaptability to changing regulations and standards, proactive risk management, and a commitment to ethical conduct.

Organizations that successfully achieve and maintain compliance are better equipped to protect sensitive information, maintain consumer trust, and navigate the complex landscape of regulations and standards.

Chapter 10: Ethical Hacking Best Practices

Ethical hacking methodologies and lifecycles provide structured approaches for conducting ethical hacking activities to identify vulnerabilities and weaknesses in an organization's systems and networks.

These methodologies guide ethical hackers, also known as penetration testers or white-hat hackers, in systematically assessing security controls and helping organizations improve their overall security posture.

One widely recognized ethical hacking methodology is the Open Web Application Security Project (OWASP) Testing Guide.

The OWASP Testing Guide outlines a comprehensive framework for testing web applications and web services for security vulnerabilities.

It covers various aspects of web application security, including authentication, authorization, input validation, and session management.

Another well-known ethical hacking methodology is the Penetration Testing Execution Standard (PTES).

PTES provides a standardized approach to conducting penetration tests, from initial planning and scoping to post-exploitation activities.

PTES emphasizes the importance of thorough documentation and reporting, helping organizations understand the security risks they face and how to address them.

The Information Systems Security Assessment Framework (ISSAF) is another ethical hacking methodology that focuses on assessing information systems for security weaknesses.

ISSAF offers guidance on conducting a wide range of security assessments, including network security, web application security, and mobile application security.

For organizations with a specific focus on wireless network security, the Wireless Penetration Testing (WPT) methodology provides a structured approach to assessing the security of wireless networks.

WPT covers topics such as wireless network discovery, enumeration, and exploitation of vulnerabilities in wireless access points and clients.

In addition to these specific methodologies, ethical hacking typically follows a common lifecycle that includes several key phases.

The first phase is "Planning and Preparation," where ethical hackers define the scope of the engagement, establish goals and objectives, and obtain necessary permissions and agreements from the organization being tested.

During this phase, ethical hackers also gather information about the target systems and networks, such as IP addresses, network diagrams, and system documentation.

The "Reconnaissance" phase involves collecting additional information about the target organization, such as publicly available data, domain names, and email addresses associated with the organization.

Ethical hackers may use various tools and techniques to gather this information, including open-source intelligence (OSINT) and passive scanning.

The "Scanning and Enumeration" phase focuses on actively scanning the target systems and networks to identify open ports, services, and potential vulnerabilities.

Ethical hackers use tools like port scanners, vulnerability scanners, and enumeration scripts to gather detailed information about the target environment.

Once potential vulnerabilities are identified, the "Vulnerability Analysis" phase involves assessing the severity and impact of each vulnerability.

Ethical hackers prioritize vulnerabilities based on their potential risk and exploitability and create a list of actionable findings.

The "Exploitation" phase is where ethical hackers attempt to exploit the identified vulnerabilities to gain unauthorized access or control over target systems.

This phase requires careful consideration of the organization's policies and agreements to ensure that ethical hacking activities do not cause harm or disruption.

After successful exploitation or a failed attempt, the ethical hackers enter the "Post-Exploitation" phase, where they assess the extent of the compromise and gather additional information or access.

This phase may involve maintaining access to the compromised systems to demonstrate the impact of the vulnerabilities.

The final phase is "Reporting and Documentation," where ethical hackers provide a detailed report of their findings to the organization.

The report typically includes information about vulnerabilities, their severity, potential risks, and recommendations for remediation.

Clear and concise reporting is crucial to help organizations understand the security risks they face and take appropriate actions to improve their security posture.

Ethical hacking methodologies and lifecycles play a vital role in helping organizations proactively identify and address security vulnerabilities.

These structured approaches provide a systematic way to assess security controls, prioritize vulnerabilities, and guide organizations in strengthening their defenses.

Ethical hackers, armed with the knowledge and methodologies, can assist organizations in identifying weaknesses before malicious hackers exploit them, ultimately enhancing cybersecurity and reducing the risk of data breaches and cyberattacks.

In summary, ethical hacking methodologies and lifecycles offer organized and systematic approaches to identifying and addressing security vulnerabilities in an organization's systems and networks.

These methodologies, such as OWASP Testing Guide, PTES, ISSAF, and WPT, provide valuable guidance for ethical hackers in conducting assessments and penetration tests.

The common ethical hacking lifecycle includes planning, reconnaissance, scanning and enumeration, vulnerability analysis, exploitation, post-exploitation, and reporting.

By following these methodologies and lifecycles, ethical hackers can help organizations strengthen their security defenses and reduce the risk of cyber threats and data breaches. Staying up-to-date with emerging threats is an essential aspect of maintaining effective cybersecurity measures in today's rapidly evolving digital landscape.

Cyber threats constantly evolve as hackers develop new techniques, exploit vulnerabilities, and target organizations with sophisticated attacks. To effectively protect against these threats, organizations must stay informed about the latest developments in the cybersecurity landscape.

One crucial source of information for staying up-to-date with emerging threats is cybersecurity news and publications.

Cybersecurity news outlets and websites regularly report on new threats, data breaches, and vulnerabilities that can impact organizations.

Subscribing to reputable cybersecurity news sources and publications can provide organizations with timely information about emerging threats and the tactics used by cybercriminals.

Additionally, organizations should follow cybersecurity experts and organizations on social media platforms to receive real-time updates and insights into the ever-changing threat landscape.

Another valuable resource for staying informed about emerging threats is information sharing and collaboration within the cybersecurity community.

Many organizations participate in information-sharing programs and forums where they can exchange threat intelligence and insights with peers and industry experts.

Collaborating with other organizations and sharing threat data can help identify emerging threats and vulnerabilities more quickly and enable proactive defenses.

In addition to external sources, organizations should also establish internal mechanisms for threat monitoring and detection.

Implementing security information and event management (SIEM) systems can help organizations monitor their network and system logs for suspicious activities and potential indicators of compromise.

SIEM solutions can correlate data from various sources and generate alerts for potential threats.

Regularly reviewing and analyzing SIEM alerts can help organizations identify and respond to emerging threats in a timely manner.

Vulnerability management programs are essential for identifying and addressing weaknesses in an organization's infrastructure and software.

Regular vulnerability scans and assessments can help organizations detect vulnerabilities before they are exploited by attackers.

Organizations should also subscribe to vulnerability databases and mailing lists to receive notifications about newly discovered vulnerabilities and available patches.

Implementing a robust patch management process is critical for promptly applying security patches to mitigate known vulnerabilities.

Regularly patching software and systems can significantly reduce the attack surface and protect against emerging threats.

Threat intelligence feeds are another valuable resource for staying informed about emerging threats.

These feeds provide organizations with real-time information about the latest malware variants, attack techniques, and indicators of compromise.

Threat intelligence can be integrated into security tools and systems to enhance threat detection and response capabilities.

Many organizations also leverage threat intelligence platforms to aggregate and analyze threat data from various sources.

Security awareness and training programs are essential for educating employees about emerging threats and promoting a security-conscious culture within the organization.

Employees should be trained to recognize phishing emails, social engineering attempts, and other tactics used by cybercriminals.

Regular training and awareness programs can help employees become an active line of defense against emerging threats.

Threat modeling is a proactive approach to identifying potential vulnerabilities and threats in an organization's systems and applications.

By conducting threat modeling exercises, organizations can assess their security posture and make informed decisions about where to allocate resources for protection against emerging threats.

Regular penetration testing and red teaming exercises can help organizations simulate real-world attacks and assess their ability to defend against emerging threats.

These exercises provide valuable insights into an organization's security weaknesses and areas that require improvement.

Security professionals should continuously improve their skills and knowledge by pursuing certifications, attending training programs, and participating in cybersecurity communities.

Cybersecurity certifications, such as Certified Information Systems Security Professional (CISSP) or Certified Ethical Hacker (CEH), can validate the expertise of security professionals and keep them up-to-date with the latest security practices and technologies.

Participating in cybersecurity communities and forums allows professionals to share experiences, exchange insights, and learn from their peers about emerging threats and best practices.

In summary, staying up-to-date with emerging threats is a critical component of maintaining effective cybersecurity defenses.

Organizations should rely on a combination of external sources, internal monitoring, vulnerability management, threat intelligence, employee training, threat modeling, and regular testing to stay informed and prepared.

By continuously adapting to the evolving threat landscape and implementing proactive security measures, organizations can reduce their exposure to emerging threats and enhance their overall cybersecurity resilience.

BOOK 3
ETHICAL HACKING UNLEASHED
ADVANCED SECURITY AUDITING TECHNIQUES

ROB BOTWRIGHT

Chapter 1: The Art of Ethical Hacking

The ethics and principles of ethical hacking form the foundation of responsible and lawful cybersecurity practices in today's digital age.

Ethical hacking, also known as penetration testing or white-hat hacking, involves authorized individuals or security professionals, known as ethical hackers, attempting to identify vulnerabilities and weaknesses in computer systems, networks, and applications.

These ethical hackers conduct their activities with the explicit permission of the organization being tested, ensuring that their actions comply with legal and ethical standards.

At the core of ethical hacking lies the principle of consent, which emphasizes the importance of obtaining permission from the organization or system owner before conducting any security assessments.

Obtaining informed and documented consent ensures that ethical hackers operate within the boundaries of the law and ethical guidelines.

Consent serves as a critical ethical safeguard, as unauthorized hacking activities are illegal and can lead to criminal charges.

Ethical hackers must adhere to strict ethical guidelines and principles to maintain their integrity and credibility within the cybersecurity community.

One of the primary ethical principles of ethical hacking is the principle of "do no harm," which emphasizes the importance of conducting security assessments without causing harm to the target systems or networks.

Ethical hackers should avoid actions that disrupt the normal operation of systems, compromise data confidentiality, or cause financial losses to the organization.

Another fundamental ethical principle is transparency, which involves open and honest communication with the organization being tested.

Ethical hackers must provide clear and accurate information about their activities, findings, and recommendations to the organization's stakeholders.

Transparency fosters trust and collaboration between ethical hackers and organizations, allowing for effective vulnerability remediation and risk management.

Furthermore, ethical hackers should maintain a high degree of professionalism and integrity in their actions and interactions.

They should act with diligence, competence, and objectivity, conducting assessments in a systematic and methodical manner.

Ethical hackers should avoid conflicts of interest and disclose any potential conflicts that may compromise their impartiality.

This commitment to professionalism and objectivity ensures that ethical hacking activities are conducted with integrity and credibility.

Ethical hackers should also respect the privacy and confidentiality of sensitive information they encounter during security assessments.

They should not disclose, share, or misuse any proprietary or confidential data discovered during their engagements.

Maintaining the confidentiality of sensitive information is crucial for maintaining trust and ethical standards.

Moreover, ethical hackers should continually update their knowledge and skills to stay current with emerging threats and evolving cybersecurity technologies.

They should engage in ongoing training and education to enhance their expertise and ensure they remain effective in their roles.

Ethical hackers often pursue certifications, such as Certified Ethical Hacker (CEH) or Offensive Security Certified Professional (OSCP), to validate their skills and knowledge.

Ethical hacking activities should always prioritize the organization's security and compliance with legal and regulatory requirements.

Ethical hackers should help organizations identify and address vulnerabilities, develop effective security measures, and achieve compliance with relevant standards and regulations.

The principle of responsible disclosure is another essential ethical consideration in ethical hacking.

If ethical hackers discover vulnerabilities that pose a significant risk, they should follow a responsible disclosure process.

This process typically involves notifying the organization of the vulnerabilities and allowing them a reasonable amount of time to address the issues before publicly disclosing them.

Responsible disclosure helps protect organizations from potential harm while promoting responsible and ethical behavior within the cybersecurity community.

In addition to responsible disclosure, ethical hackers should adhere to the principles of non-repudiation and traceability.

Non-repudiation ensures that ethical hackers maintain records and evidence of their activities, which can be used to verify their actions and findings.

Traceability allows organizations to trace the actions of ethical hackers and validate the legitimacy of their activities.

Ethical hacking engagements should be well-documented, with comprehensive reports detailing the vulnerabilities discovered, their severity, and recommendations for remediation.

These reports serve as essential tools for organizations to improve their security posture and mitigate risks effectively.

Ethical hackers should communicate their findings and recommendations in a clear and understandable manner, avoiding technical jargon and providing actionable guidance.

Moreover, ethical hackers should maintain a commitment to continuous improvement and collaboration with organizations to enhance security measures.

They should view ethical hacking as a partnership with the organization, working together to achieve the common goal of protecting digital assets and data.

Overall, the ethics and principles of ethical hacking are integral to ensuring that security assessments are conducted responsibly, lawfully, and ethically.

Ethical hackers play a vital role in helping organizations identify and address security vulnerabilities, strengthen their defenses, and navigate the ever-changing cybersecurity landscape.

By upholding ethical standards, maintaining transparency, and prioritizing the security of organizations, ethical hackers contribute to a safer digital environment for all.

Building a successful ethical hacking career is an exciting and rewarding journey in the field of cybersecurity.

As organizations increasingly rely on digital technologies and the internet, the demand for skilled ethical hackers has grown significantly.

To embark on a successful ethical hacking career, one must first develop a strong foundation in information security concepts and practices.

Understanding the fundamentals of network security, cryptography, operating systems, and programming languages is essential for ethical hackers.

Many aspiring ethical hackers begin their journey by pursuing relevant certifications, such as CompTIA Security+, Certified Information Systems Security Professional (CISSP), or Certified Ethical Hacker (CEH).

These certifications provide a structured learning path and validate the knowledge and skills required for ethical hacking roles.

In addition to formal education and certifications, ethical hackers should possess a curious and inquisitive mindset.

The ability to think creatively and critically is invaluable when it comes to identifying vulnerabilities and devising effective solutions.

Ethical hackers often face complex and challenging scenarios that require problem-solving skills and adaptability.

Aspiring ethical hackers should also cultivate strong communication skills, both written and verbal.

The ability to convey technical information in a clear and understandable manner is crucial when reporting vulnerabilities and collaborating with organizational stakeholders.

Furthermore, ethical hackers should keep pace with emerging threats and evolving technologies by staying updated through continuous learning and industry research.

Cybersecurity is a dynamic field, and staying current is essential for success.

To gain practical experience, ethical hackers can participate in capture the flag (CTF) competitions, engage in bug bounty programs, or set up their own lab environments for hands-on practice.

CTF competitions and bug bounty programs offer opportunities to test and apply skills in real-world scenarios while earning rewards for identifying vulnerabilities.

Creating a lab environment allows ethical hackers to experiment with different tools, techniques, and configurations in a controlled setting.

Ethical hackers should also be familiar with various hacking tools and technologies commonly used in penetration testing and vulnerability assessments.

Tools like Nmap, Wireshark, Metasploit, and Burp Suite are essential for conducting ethical hacking activities effectively.

Moreover, ethical hackers should have a strong understanding of the legal and ethical aspects of their work.

Ethical hacking should always be performed with the explicit permission and consent of the organization being tested.

Unauthorized hacking activities are illegal and can lead to severe legal consequences.

Ethical hackers should document their engagements meticulously, ensuring that all actions are transparent, traceable, and aligned with ethical guidelines.

Building a successful ethical hacking career often involves specialization in specific areas of cybersecurity.

Ethical hackers can choose to focus on network security, web application security, mobile security, cloud security, or other specialized domains.

Specialization allows ethical hackers to develop expertise and in-depth knowledge in their chosen field, making them valuable assets to organizations.

Ethical hackers should also consider obtaining additional certifications and advanced training in their chosen specialization.

Certifications like Offensive Security Certified Professional (OSCP) for penetration testing or Certified Web Application Tester (CWAPT) for web application security can further enhance career prospects.

Networking is another essential aspect of building a successful ethical hacking career.

Engaging with the cybersecurity community through conferences, forums, and online platforms allows ethical hackers to connect with peers, share knowledge, and stay updated on industry trends.

Mentorship can also play a significant role in career development.

Seeking guidance from experienced professionals in the field can provide valuable insights, career advice, and opportunities for growth.

Furthermore, ethical hackers should explore various career paths within the cybersecurity field.

They can pursue roles such as penetration tester, security consultant, security analyst, incident responder, or security researcher.

Each role offers unique challenges and opportunities for career advancement.

To stand out in the competitive field of ethical hacking, professionals should consider contributing to the cybersecurity community by publishing research, sharing knowledge, or participating in open-source projects.

Contributions to the community demonstrate expertise and commitment to the field, enhancing professional reputation.

Ethical hackers should continuously assess and improve their skills and knowledge through ongoing training and education.

Cybersecurity threats evolve rapidly, and staying ahead of attackers requires a commitment to lifelong learning.

Building a successful ethical hacking career is not only about technical expertise but also about professionalism, ethics, and a dedication to protecting digital assets and data.

Ethical hackers play a crucial role in helping organizations defend against cyber threats and secure their information systems.

Ultimately, a successful ethical hacking career is built on a foundation of knowledge, experience, ethics, and a passion for making the digital world safer for all.

Chapter 2: Advanced Reconnaissance Strategies

Leveraging open-source intelligence (OSINT) is a fundamental aspect of conducting in-depth reconnaissance for various purposes, including cybersecurity, investigations, and threat analysis.

OSINT refers to the collection and analysis of publicly available information from sources such as the internet, social media, public records, and other publicly accessible repositories.

OSINT provides valuable insights into an organization, individual, or entity, enabling informed decision-making and a deeper understanding of the target.

One of the primary benefits of OSINT is its accessibility, as it relies on publicly available information that does not require unauthorized access or hacking.

However, OSINT requires skilled researchers who can effectively gather, analyze, and interpret the vast amount of data available on the internet.

Effective OSINT involves a structured and systematic approach, starting with defining the objectives and scope of the reconnaissance.

Researchers must clearly outline what information they seek and how it will be used, ensuring that the OSINT activities align with ethical and legal guidelines.

To conduct OSINT effectively, researchers rely on a variety of tools and techniques tailored to their specific goals.

Search engines are a fundamental tool in OSINT, allowing researchers to query keywords, phrases, and domains to discover relevant information.

Advanced search operators and modifiers can help refine search results and uncover hidden or specific details.

Social media platforms are rich sources of OSINT, as they often contain a wealth of personal and organizational information.

Researchers can analyze social media profiles, posts, and connections to gather insights about individuals, their interests, relationships, and activities.

In addition to general search engines, specialized search engines and databases designed for OSINT, such as Shodan and Censys, provide access to information about internet-connected devices, services, and infrastructure.

Domain Name System (DNS) records, WHOIS databases, and internet registries offer valuable information about domain ownership, IP addresses, and network infrastructure.

Publicly accessible databases, government records, and online directories provide details about businesses, individuals, and organizations, including contact information, financial records, and legal filings.

Researchers can use web scraping and data mining techniques to extract structured data from websites, forums, and online publications.

OSINT also encompasses the analysis of metadata, which includes information embedded in files, documents, and images.

Metadata can reveal details about the creation, modification, and distribution of digital content.

Geolocation data, such as GPS coordinates embedded in photos or social media posts, can help pinpoint the physical locations associated with targets.

While OSINT is a powerful tool for gathering information, it is essential to consider the ethical and legal implications of data collection and analysis.

Researchers must adhere to privacy and data protection laws and regulations, respecting individuals' rights and avoiding the use of unauthorized or non-public information.

Ethical considerations include the responsible handling of sensitive data and the avoidance of harassment, doxxing, or other harmful actions.

In-depth reconnaissance using OSINT often involves profiling targets to build comprehensive profiles that aid in understanding their digital footprint and potential vulnerabilities.

Profiling includes collecting information about an entity's online presence, social media activity, affiliations, and historical data.

Analyzing patterns and trends within the collected data can reveal valuable insights, such as potential security weaknesses, threat actors, or indicators of compromise.

OSINT plays a critical role in cybersecurity by helping organizations identify and assess their online exposure and potential attack vectors.

By monitoring and analyzing OSINT sources, security teams can stay informed about emerging threats, vulnerabilities, and tactics used by malicious actors.

Effective OSINT can assist in threat intelligence, risk assessment, and incident response.

For investigative purposes, OSINT can provide valuable leads, evidence, and background information.

Law enforcement agencies, private investigators, and journalists often rely on OSINT to support their investigations and reporting.

In the context of competitive intelligence, OSINT can help organizations gather information about competitors, market trends, and industry developments.

Strategic decision-making benefits from a thorough understanding of the competitive landscape.

OSINT is also a valuable tool for threat intelligence analysts who track the activities and capabilities of threat actors, such as cybercriminals and nation-state adversaries.

Regular OSINT monitoring can reveal signs of impending cyberattacks, data breaches, or other malicious activities.

In the realm of risk management, OSINT assists organizations in identifying and mitigating potential risks associated with partners, suppliers, and third-party vendors.

Understanding the digital reputation and security posture of third parties is essential for maintaining a secure supply chain.

While OSINT provides numerous advantages, it is essential to be aware of its limitations.

Publicly available information may not always be accurate, up-to-date, or comprehensive.

Additionally, the availability of certain information may vary by region or country due to legal and cultural differences.

Furthermore, OSINT should be complemented by other intelligence sources, such as human intelligence (HUMINT), signals intelligence (SIGINT), and technical intelligence (TECHINT), for a more holistic view of threats and opportunities.

In summary, leveraging OSINT for in-depth reconnaissance is a valuable and ethical practice that empowers individuals, organizations, and security professionals to gather insights, mitigate risks, and make informed decisions in an increasingly interconnected world.

By employing OSINT tools and techniques responsibly and within legal boundaries, researchers can uncover valuable information and contribute to enhanced cybersecurity, investigations, and strategic planning.

Advanced footprinting and target profiling are essential techniques in the realm of information gathering and reconnaissance, allowing individuals, organizations, and security professionals to gain in-depth insights into their targets.

Footprinting involves the systematic collection of information about a target, which can be an individual, organization, or system, with the goal of creating a comprehensive profile.

In advanced footprinting, the focus extends beyond basic data gathering, encompassing a more sophisticated and detailed approach to reconnaissance.

This advanced approach considers multiple data sources, techniques, and analysis methods to build a nuanced understanding of the target.

One of the primary objectives of advanced footprinting is to identify potential vulnerabilities and weaknesses that could be exploited by malicious actors or addressed by security professionals.

While the term "footprinting" may evoke the image of physical footprints, in the digital realm, it refers to the traces and indicators left by an entity's online activities and presence.

These digital footprints include a wide range of information, such as domain names, IP addresses, email addresses, subdomains, social media profiles, and more.

The initial step in advanced footprinting is to define the scope and objectives of the reconnaissance effort, clarifying what information is sought and how it will be used.

A well-defined scope helps researchers focus their efforts and ensures that the footprinting activities remain within ethical and legal boundaries.

Open-source intelligence (OSINT) is a valuable resource for advanced footprinting, providing access to publicly available information from a variety of sources.

OSINT encompasses data from the internet, social media, public records, online forums, websites, and more.

Researchers use OSINT tools and techniques to query search engines, analyze websites, and scrape data from online platforms, collecting information relevant to the target.

Advanced footprinting may involve the use of specialized OSINT tools and search engines, such as Shodan, Censys, Maltego, and others, to uncover technical details about the target's internet infrastructure.

Researchers can also explore domain registration information through WHOIS databases and DNS records to discover details about domain ownership, registration dates, and contact information.

In addition to technical details, advanced footprinting delves into the target's digital presence on social media platforms, including profiles, connections, posts, and interactions.

Analyzing social media content can provide insights into an individual's interests, affiliations, relationships, and activities.

Furthermore, advanced footprinting extends to email footprinting, which involves the collection and analysis of email addresses associated with the target.

Email addresses can reveal valuable information, such as the target's communication patterns, organizational affiliations, and potential points of contact.

Subdomain enumeration is another critical aspect of advanced footprinting, as subdomains can often lead to overlooked entry points or vulnerabilities in a target's network.

Advanced footprinting tools and techniques can identify subdomains associated with the target's domain, helping researchers expand their understanding of the target's online presence.

Target profiling is the natural progression of advanced footprinting, where the collected information is organized, analyzed, and synthesized to create a comprehensive profile of the target.

This profile may include technical details, digital footprints, social connections, affiliations, interests, and other relevant information.

Analyzing the collected data often involves pattern recognition, data correlation, and the identification of potential security risks.

Researchers may use data visualization tools and techniques to represent the information in a meaningful way, aiding in the identification of trends, relationships, and potential vulnerabilities.

The objective of target profiling is to provide decision-makers with actionable intelligence that can inform security measures, risk assessments, and strategic planning.

For security professionals, target profiling assists in identifying potential attack vectors, vulnerabilities, and areas requiring enhanced protection.

It allows organizations to proactively address security risks and deploy appropriate defenses.

In threat intelligence and cybersecurity, target profiling plays a crucial role in understanding the motivations, capabilities, and tactics of potential threat actors.

Profiling threat actors helps security teams anticipate and defend against specific threats, such as cyberattacks, espionage, or insider threats.

To ensure the ethical and legal use of advanced footprinting and target profiling, researchers must adhere to privacy and data protection laws, as well as ethical guidelines.

Respecting individuals' rights to privacy and obtaining proper consent for data collection are essential considerations.

Advanced footprinting and target profiling should be conducted transparently and within the boundaries of the law.

Furthermore, the information gathered should be handled responsibly and securely to prevent unauthorized access or disclosure.

In summary, advanced footprinting and target profiling are indispensable techniques for information gathering and reconnaissance in various domains, including cybersecurity, investigations, and threat analysis.

These techniques provide valuable insights into targets, allowing individuals and organizations to make informed decisions, enhance security, and mitigate risks effectively.

When used responsibly and ethically, advanced footprinting and target profiling contribute to a safer and more secure digital environment for all.

Chapter 3: Exploiting Security Weaknesses

Identifying and exploiting zero-day vulnerabilities is a complex and controversial topic within the realm of cybersecurity, raising ethical, legal, and practical considerations.

Zero-day vulnerabilities are software flaws or weaknesses that are unknown to the software vendor and have not been patched or fixed.

These vulnerabilities are called "zero-day" because there are zero days of protection from the moment they are discovered by malicious actors until they are addressed by the vendor.

The discovery and exploitation of zero-day vulnerabilities can have significant implications for both attackers and defenders in the cybersecurity landscape.

On one hand, zero-day vulnerabilities are highly sought after by cybercriminals, nation-state actors, and other malicious entities because they provide a potent weapon for launching attacks against individuals, organizations, and critical infrastructure.

On the other hand, the responsible disclosure and patching of zero-day vulnerabilities are essential for enhancing cybersecurity and protecting users.

The ethical considerations surrounding zero-day vulnerabilities revolve around the dilemma of whether and how to disclose such vulnerabilities to the affected software vendors.

Responsible disclosure is the practice of reporting the vulnerability to the vendor or developer and giving them a reasonable amount of time to develop and release a patch before the vulnerability is publicly disclosed.

This approach aims to minimize the potential harm caused by the vulnerability while allowing the vendor to address the issue.

However, some ethical hackers and security researchers face challenges when attempting to responsibly disclose zero-day vulnerabilities.

Concerns about legal repercussions, lack of vendor responsiveness, or the potential for the vulnerability to be exploited by others may influence their decision-making.

In some cases, security researchers may choose to sell or share zero-day vulnerabilities with government agencies, private companies, or cybersecurity firms, raising additional ethical questions about the responsible use of such knowledge.

Governments and intelligence agencies may use zero-day vulnerabilities for espionage, surveillance, or cyber operations, further complicating the ethical landscape.

The legal aspects of identifying and exploiting zero-day vulnerabilities also vary by jurisdiction.

Some countries have laws that criminalize the unauthorized discovery or exploitation of vulnerabilities, while others may have more permissive or ambiguous legal frameworks.

Navigating these legal considerations requires a deep understanding of the laws in place and the potential consequences for ethical hackers and security researchers.

From a practical perspective, identifying zero-day vulnerabilities often requires a combination of skills, including reverse engineering, vulnerability analysis, and advanced penetration testing techniques.

Security researchers may use tools and methods to analyze software binaries, system memory, and network traffic to uncover previously unknown weaknesses.

Exploiting zero-day vulnerabilities typically involves crafting and deploying malicious code or techniques that take advantage of the vulnerability to gain unauthorized access, execute arbitrary code, or achieve other malicious goals.

The development of zero-day exploits is a highly specialized skill that requires a deep understanding of software internals and exploitation techniques.

Zero-day vulnerabilities can target a wide range of software and systems, including operating systems, web browsers, server software, and mobile applications.

The impact of a successful zero-day exploit can range from unauthorized data access to system compromise and control.

Mitigating the risks associated with zero-day vulnerabilities requires a multi-faceted approach.

Software vendors and developers play a critical role in reducing the window of vulnerability by promptly addressing and patching reported vulnerabilities.

Users and organizations must apply patches and updates in a timely manner to protect their systems and data.

Additionally, the use of security measures such as intrusion detection systems, network segmentation, and application whitelisting can help mitigate the impact of zero-day exploits.

The responsible disclosure of zero-day vulnerabilities by security researchers is essential for enhancing overall cybersecurity.

Many security researchers and organizations have established guidelines and best practices for responsible disclosure, which typically involve notifying the affected vendor, providing technical details, and allowing a reasonable time frame for patch development.

While the debate over the ethics and practices of identifying and exploiting zero-day vulnerabilities continues, the need for responsible disclosure and collaboration between ethical hackers, security researchers, vendors, and organizations remains paramount.

Ultimately, the ethical considerations, legal constraints, and practical challenges surrounding zero-day vulnerabilities underscore the complex and evolving nature of cybersecurity in a digital world where knowledge and vulnerabilities can be both a weapon and a shield.

Social engineering techniques and exploits are deceptive and manipulative tactics used by malicious actors to manipulate individuals into divulging confidential information, performing actions against their best interests, or providing unauthorized access to systems and data.

These techniques prey on human psychology and behavior, exploiting cognitive biases, trust, and social norms to achieve their objectives.

Social engineering attacks are not limited to the digital realm and can manifest in various forms, including in-person interactions, phone calls, email, and online messaging.

One common social engineering tactic is phishing, where attackers craft deceptive emails or messages that appear legitimate, often mimicking trusted organizations or individuals, to trick recipients into clicking on malicious links or downloading malware.

Another variant of phishing is spear-phishing, which targets specific individuals or organizations, often with personalized and convincing messages.

Pretexting is a social engineering technique in which attackers create a fabricated scenario or pretext to gain the trust of their target, convincing them to divulge sensitive information or perform actions they otherwise wouldn't.

In pretexting scenarios, attackers may pose as trusted entities, such as technical support personnel or colleagues, to manipulate the target into providing access or information.

Baiting involves enticing a target with the promise of something valuable, such as free software, a download, or a physical object, to encourage them to take a specific action, like clicking on a malicious link or opening an infected file.

Quid pro quo is a social engineering technique where an attacker offers something of value to the target in exchange for sensitive information or access.

For example, an attacker may pose as an IT technician offering tech support in return for login credentials.

Tailgating, also known as piggybacking, involves an attacker physically following a legitimate employee into a secure area without proper authorization, taking advantage of the trust extended to employees.

Impersonation is a social engineering tactic in which attackers impersonate trusted individuals, often through email or phone calls, to manipulate the target into providing information or access.

Vishing, or voice phishing, relies on phone calls to deceive targets into disclosing sensitive information, such as credit card numbers or login credentials.

Vishing attacks may use caller ID spoofing to appear more convincing.

Pharming is a social engineering technique in which attackers manipulate the Domain Name System (DNS) or hosts file to redirect users to fraudulent websites, where they may unwittingly provide sensitive information.

Social engineering exploits leverage human emotions and vulnerabilities, including fear, curiosity, trust, and urgency, to increase their chances of success.

Attackers often create a sense of urgency or fear to pressure the target into immediate action, such as clicking on a link or revealing information.

Social engineers may also exploit individuals' curiosity by crafting intriguing or enticing messages that prompt recipients to take actions they would otherwise avoid.

In many social engineering attacks, attackers use information gathered from open-source intelligence (OSINT) to personalize their approaches, making their messages or requests more convincing.

Social engineering exploits have been used in a wide range of attacks, including data breaches, account takeovers, identity theft, and financial fraud.

Defending against social engineering attacks requires a combination of awareness, education, and technical safeguards.

Employee training and awareness programs can help individuals recognize common social engineering tactics and develop the skepticism needed to verify requests and messages.

Organizations should implement strong authentication methods, including multi-factor authentication (MFA), to reduce the risk of unauthorized access even if credentials are compromised.

Security policies and procedures should address social engineering risks and provide guidelines for verifying identities and information requests.

Email filtering and spam detection systems can help identify and quarantine phishing and malicious emails, reducing the likelihood of successful attacks.

Individuals should be cautious when receiving unsolicited messages or requests for sensitive information, especially if they create a sense of urgency or seem too good to be true.

Verifying the legitimacy of requests, such as by contacting the requesting party through official channels, can help prevent falling victim to social engineering exploits.

Additionally, organizations can use intrusion detection systems (IDS) and security information and event management (SIEM) solutions to monitor network traffic and detect suspicious activities associated with social engineering attacks.

While technical defenses are essential, the human element remains a critical factor in defending against social engineering exploits.

Security awareness, vigilance, and skepticism can go a long way in thwarting these deceptive tactics and protecting individuals and organizations from the potential consequences of falling victim to social engineering attacks.

In an increasingly connected and digital world, where information is a valuable commodity, staying informed and vigilant is key to mitigating the risks posed by social engineering techniques and exploits.

Chapter 4: Mastering Penetration Testing

Advanced attack vectors and techniques represent the cutting edge of cyber threats, continually evolving to bypass traditional security measures and exploit vulnerabilities in increasingly sophisticated ways.

These vectors and techniques pose significant challenges to individuals, organizations, and cybersecurity professionals, demanding a proactive and adaptive approach to defense.

One of the advanced attack vectors that has gained prominence in recent years is fileless malware, a type of malicious software that operates entirely in memory, leaving little to no trace on the victim's system.

Fileless malware leverages legitimate system tools and processes to carry out attacks, making it difficult to detect and mitigate using traditional antivirus solutions.

Attackers often use fileless malware to achieve objectives such as data theft, espionage, or the deployment of additional malicious payloads.

Another advanced attack vector is known as living-off-the-land (LOL) attacks, where attackers exploit legitimate applications, utilities, and scripts already present on a victim's system to carry out malicious activities.

LOL attacks aim to blend in with normal system behavior, making it challenging for security solutions to differentiate between legitimate and malicious activities.

These attacks can involve abusing PowerShell, Windows Management Instrumentation (WMI), or other trusted tools to execute malicious code.

Fileless malware and LOL attacks are particularly challenging because they operate without the need for malicious files, making traditional signature-based detection methods less effective.

Another advanced technique that cybercriminals employ is polymorphic malware, which continually changes its code and appearance to evade detection.

Polymorphic malware can alter its characteristics with each infection, making it difficult for antivirus solutions to identify and block.

This technique allows attackers to create malware that can bypass signature-based defenses, adapt to different environments, and maintain persistence on compromised systems.

Advanced attackers often use privilege escalation techniques to elevate their access rights on a compromised system.

Privilege escalation exploits vulnerabilities or misconfigurations in the operating system or software to gain higher levels of access, enabling the attacker to perform more intrusive actions.

Privilege escalation can lead to the compromise of critical system components, potentially resulting in system-wide compromise and data breaches.

Spear-phishing campaigns represent another advanced attack vector, targeting specific individuals or organizations with highly customized and convincing messages.

These messages often leverage carefully researched information to deceive the recipient into taking actions that could lead to malware infection or data disclosure.

Spear-phishing campaigns can be used as entry points for more extensive attacks, such as advanced persistent threats (APTs) that aim to establish long-term access and control over a target's network.

To evade detection and monitoring, advanced attackers employ techniques like anti-forensics, which involve manipulating or erasing digital evidence of their activities.

This can include modifying log files, altering timestamps, or using encryption and steganography to hide malicious payloads and communications.

Anti-forensics tactics make it challenging for incident responders and digital forensic analysts to reconstruct the timeline and details of an attack.

Cryptomining malware, also known as cryptojacking, is another advanced attack vector that has gained prominence.

In these attacks, malicious actors compromise systems to mine cryptocurrencies without the owner's consent, often consuming significant computational resources and energy.

Cryptomining malware can slow down affected systems, increase operational costs, and disrupt business operations.

Advanced attack techniques also encompass supply chain attacks, where attackers compromise trusted suppliers or distributors to gain access to their customers' systems.

Supply chain attacks can be highly effective, as they target systems that are trusted and have legitimate access.

The SolarWinds breach, for example, exemplified the significant impact supply chain attacks can have on organizations and even governments.

Zero-day exploits are advanced techniques that target vulnerabilities unknown to the software vendor and, therefore, unpatched.

Attackers who discover zero-day vulnerabilities can exploit them to gain unauthorized access, execute arbitrary code, or achieve other malicious objectives.

Zero-day exploits are highly coveted by advanced attackers and can fetch substantial prices on the black market.

To defend against advanced attack vectors and techniques, organizations and individuals must adopt a multi-layered security approach that includes proactive threat hunting, user education, endpoint protection, and network monitoring.

Behavior-based detection mechanisms, such as anomaly detection and machine learning, can help identify abnormal activities associated with advanced attacks.

Security teams should also stay informed about emerging threats and vulnerabilities, continually update security measures, and conduct penetration testing to identify and remediate weaknesses.

Additionally, organizations should implement strong access controls, network segmentation, and least privilege principles to limit the impact of successful attacks.

Collaboration within the cybersecurity community and sharing threat intelligence can help organizations stay ahead of evolving threats and enhance their overall security posture.

In summary, advanced attack vectors and techniques represent an ongoing challenge in the ever-evolving landscape of cybersecurity.

As attackers become more sophisticated, defenders must adapt by employing advanced security measures, threat intelligence sharing, and a proactive mindset to protect against these evolving threats.

Post-exploitation and evasion strategies are critical components of advanced cyberattacks, allowing attackers to maintain control over compromised systems and evade detection by security defenses.

Once an attacker has successfully breached a target's defenses and gained access to a system or network, the post-exploitation phase begins, and the focus shifts to achieving the attacker's goals while avoiding detection and removal.

One fundamental post-exploitation strategy is establishing persistence, which involves maintaining unauthorized access to the compromised system or network even after the initial breach.

Persistence mechanisms can be hardware-based, such as inserting malicious hardware devices, or software-based, where the attacker deploys backdoors, rootkits, or Trojans to ensure ongoing access.

To achieve persistence, attackers may modify system configurations, schedule tasks, or create hidden user accounts, making it challenging for defenders to identify and remove their presence.

Evasion techniques are used to hide malicious activities and avoid triggering alarms or suspicion.

Attackers employ various evasion methods to evade detection, including obfuscating malicious code, disguising network traffic, and bypassing security mechanisms.

One common evasion tactic is the use of encryption to conceal malicious communication.

By encrypting data and using secure protocols, attackers can make it difficult for network monitoring solutions to inspect and detect their activities.

Another evasion technique involves using legitimate system utilities and processes to carry out malicious actions, making it appear as normal system behavior.

For example, attackers may abuse PowerShell or Windows Management Instrumentation (WMI) to execute commands and exfiltrate data, blending in with legitimate administrative tasks.

Anti-forensic techniques are employed to cover tracks and erase evidence of the attacker's activities.

These techniques may involve deleting log files, altering timestamps, or overwriting data remnants to make it challenging for incident responders and forensic analysts to reconstruct the attack timeline and identify the attacker.

Privilege escalation is a post-exploitation tactic where attackers seek to gain additional privileges or permissions on the compromised system.

By elevating their access rights, attackers can perform more intrusive actions and move laterally within the network to reach higher-value targets.

Credential harvesting is a common strategy used by attackers to collect usernames and passwords from compromised systems.

Attackers may use techniques like keylogging, credential dumping, or password spraying to steal login credentials, which can be used for further attacks or lateral movement.

Lateral movement is the process of moving laterally within a network to explore and compromise additional systems and resources.

Attackers may use stolen credentials, vulnerabilities, or backdoors to traverse the network, spreading their influence and achieving their objectives.

Data exfiltration is a critical post-exploitation goal for attackers, as it involves stealing sensitive information or intellectual property from the victim's environment.

Attackers employ various methods for data exfiltration, such as transferring files over encrypted channels, hiding data within legitimate traffic, or leveraging cloud storage services to store stolen information.

Post-exploitation and evasion strategies often go hand in hand, as attackers seek to maintain their presence on compromised systems while avoiding detection.

Defenders must employ advanced security measures to detect and respond to these strategies effectively.

Behavior-based detection mechanisms, such as anomaly detection and machine learning, can help identify abnormal activities associated with post-exploitation and evasion.

Endpoint detection and response (EDR) solutions are valuable for monitoring and responding to suspicious behavior on compromised systems.

Network segmentation and access controls can limit lateral movement within a network, making it more challenging for attackers to reach critical assets.

Threat hunting, a proactive approach to searching for signs of compromise, can help security teams identify post-exploitation activities early in an attack.

Additionally, organizations should maintain comprehensive incident response plans and conduct tabletop exercises to prepare for post-exploitation scenarios.

In summary, post-exploitation and evasion strategies are essential components of advanced cyberattacks, enabling attackers to achieve their goals while remaining hidden from defenders.

Defending against these strategies requires a combination of advanced detection mechanisms, proactive threat hunting, robust access controls, and a well-prepared incident response strategy.

In an ever-evolving cybersecurity landscape, staying ahead of post-exploitation and evasion tactics is crucial to maintaining the security and integrity of organizational systems and data.

Chapter 5: Web Application Security Assessment

The Open Web Application Security Project (OWASP) Top Ten is a well-recognized and influential list of the most critical web application security vulnerabilities.

These vulnerabilities pose significant risks to web applications and their users, making them a top priority for security professionals and developers.

Understanding these vulnerabilities in-depth is crucial for effectively securing web applications and mitigating potential threats.

The first vulnerability on the OWASP Top Ten list is Injection.

Injection vulnerabilities occur when untrusted data is sent to an interpreter as part of a command or query, leading to malicious code execution.

Common types of injection attacks include SQL injection and Command injection.

SQL injection involves an attacker inserting malicious SQL statements into input fields to manipulate a database.

Developers can prevent SQL injection by using parameterized queries and input validation.

The second vulnerability is Broken Authentication.

Broken Authentication vulnerabilities occur when authentication and session management are not implemented securely, enabling attackers to compromise user accounts and gain unauthorized access.

Common issues include weak password policies, session fixation, and inadequate logout mechanisms.

Implementing strong authentication mechanisms and using secure session management techniques can mitigate these vulnerabilities.

The third vulnerability is Sensitive Data Exposure.

Sensitive Data Exposure vulnerabilities occur when an application does not adequately protect sensitive data, such as credit card numbers or user passwords.

Attackers can exploit these vulnerabilities to steal or manipulate sensitive information.

Encrypting data at rest and in transit, using secure key management, and following security best practices can protect against data exposure.

The fourth vulnerability is XML External Entity (XXE) Attacks.

XXE vulnerabilities occur when an application processes XML input from untrusted sources without proper validation.

Attackers can exploit these vulnerabilities to access internal files, perform remote code execution, and carry out denial-of-service attacks.

Developers should disable external entity references in XML processors and validate XML input to prevent XXE attacks.

The fifth vulnerability is Broken Access Control.

Broken Access Control vulnerabilities occur when an application fails to enforce proper access controls, allowing unauthorized users to access restricted resources.

Common issues include missing authorization checks and insecure direct object references.

Implementing access control mechanisms and enforcing proper authorization can prevent these vulnerabilities.

The sixth vulnerability is Security Misconfigurations.

Security Misconfigurations vulnerabilities occur when an application, server, or database is not configured securely.

Attackers can exploit these vulnerabilities to access sensitive data or execute arbitrary code.

Regular security assessments, automated scanning tools, and following security best practices can help identify and remediate misconfigurations.

The seventh vulnerability is Cross-Site Scripting (XSS).

XSS vulnerabilities occur when an application includes untrusted data in web pages that are subsequently executed by a user's browser.

Attackers can inject malicious scripts, steal cookies, and perform actions on behalf of the user.

Developers should sanitize user input and use output encoding to prevent XSS attacks.

The eighth vulnerability is Insecure Deserialization.

Insecure Deserialization vulnerabilities occur when an application deserializes untrusted data without proper validation.

Attackers can exploit these vulnerabilities to execute arbitrary code, perform denial-of-service attacks, or gain remote control.

Developers should avoid insecure deserialization by using safe serialization formats and validating serialized data.

The ninth vulnerability is Using Components with Known Vulnerabilities.

Using outdated or vulnerable components, such as libraries and frameworks, can expose an application to security risks.

Attackers can exploit known vulnerabilities in these components to compromise the application.

Regularly updating and patching components, monitoring for security advisories, and performing code reviews can mitigate this risk.

The tenth vulnerability is Insufficient Logging and Monitoring.

Insufficient Logging and Monitoring vulnerabilities occur when an application does not adequately log security events or lacks real-time monitoring.

This can make it challenging to detect and respond to security incidents promptly.

Implementing robust logging and monitoring solutions and establishing an incident response plan are essential for addressing this vulnerability.

In summary, a comprehensive understanding of the OWASP Top Ten vulnerabilities is critical for building secure web applications.

Developers and security professionals must work together to identify, mitigate, and prevent these vulnerabilities to protect sensitive data and maintain the integrity of web applications.

Web Application Firewalls (WAFs) are crucial components of modern web application security, designed to protect web applications from a wide range of threats, including SQL injection, cross-site scripting (XSS), and other common attacks.

WAFs operate as a protective layer between the web application and the internet, inspecting incoming and outgoing traffic for malicious content and patterns.

They use a combination of signature-based rules, heuristics, and anomaly detection to identify and block potentially harmful requests.

WAFs can be an effective security measure, but like any technology, they are not immune to evasion techniques and bypass methods employed by determined attackers.

To understand how attackers bypass WAFs, it's essential to explore various evasion techniques and mitigation strategies.

One common method employed by attackers to evade WAFs is input encoding.

Attackers may use various character encoding schemes, such as percent-encoding or Unicode encoding, to obfuscate malicious payloads and bypass signature-based detection rules.

For example, encoding the '<' character as '%3C' or '\u003C' can deceive the WAF into allowing potentially harmful input.

To counter this evasion technique, security practitioners must implement proper input validation and decoding routines to ensure that incoming data is properly sanitized before processing.

Another evasion technique involves using mixed-case and obfuscated keywords.

Attackers may employ case variations and obscure keywords to disguise malicious intent.

For instance, they might use 'sElEcT' instead of 'SELECT' in SQL injection attacks or employ non-standard characters in place of regular ones.

To mitigate this technique, WAFs should be configured to perform case-insensitive matching and detect patterns that account for character substitutions.

HTTP parameter pollution (HPP) is another technique used to confuse WAFs.

In an HPP attack, an attacker injects multiple values into a single parameter, tricking the application and WAF into interpreting the data differently.

This can lead to security bypasses and unexpected behavior.

To prevent HPP, developers should validate and sanitize input at the application level and implement strong WAF configurations that detect and block such attacks.

Attackers may also employ evasion techniques involving multipart requests.

By splitting malicious payloads across multiple parts of a multipart request, attackers can evade WAF detection, as it may only analyze individual parts rather than the entire request.

To address this, WAFs should reconstruct and analyze entire multipart requests to detect hidden threats.

Additionally, attackers may use various encoding and character sets, such as UTF-7, UTF-16, or base64, to obscure malicious payloads and bypass signature-based WAF rules.

To counter this technique, WAFs should be configured to normalize and decode input consistently before analysis.

Evasion techniques may also involve encoding payloads within images or other media files, leveraging the Content-Type header to deceive WAFs into permitting malicious content.

This approach can be challenging to detect, requiring advanced content analysis and inspection capabilities in the WAF.

To defend against such attacks, organizations should implement strict content-type validation and perform deep content inspection when necessary.

Some attackers may employ timing-based evasion techniques, introducing delays between requests to evade rate limiting and detection mechanisms.

To combat this, WAFs should be configured to detect and block requests with unusual timing patterns.

Security practitioners should also monitor for rate-limiting bypass attempts and implement additional security controls when necessary.

Attackers may craft malicious requests that exploit known WAF vulnerabilities or misconfigurations, allowing them to bypass security measures altogether.

To prevent this, organizations should regularly update and patch their WAFs, perform security assessments, and follow best practices for WAF configuration and management.

In summary, while Web Application Firewalls (WAFs) play a crucial role in protecting web applications from various threats, they are not foolproof and can be bypassed by determined attackers using various evasion techniques.

To enhance their effectiveness, security professionals must continually update and configure WAFs, implement proper input validation, and employ advanced content analysis and inspection capabilities.

Combining WAFs with other security measures, such as intrusion detection systems (IDS) and threat intelligence feeds, can further strengthen an organization's defense against web application attacks and bypass techniques.

Chapter 6: Advanced Wireless Network Security

Cracking WPA3 encryption and beyond represents a significant challenge for security professionals and attackers alike in the ever-evolving landscape of wireless network security.

WPA3, introduced as the latest generation of Wi-Fi security protocols, aimed to address vulnerabilities found in its predecessor, WPA2.

WPA3 employs stronger encryption algorithms, making it more resistant to brute force and dictionary attacks.

However, no encryption method is entirely invulnerable, and as technology advances, so do the tools and techniques available to attackers.

One of the primary goals of cracking WPA3 encryption is to gain unauthorized access to a protected Wi-Fi network.

Attackers may have various motives, such as eavesdropping on network traffic, stealing sensitive information, or launching further attacks on connected devices.

Cracking WPA3 encryption typically involves attempting to discover the pre-shared key (PSK) or passphrase used to secure the network.

To achieve this, attackers use a combination of offline and online attacks, depending on the network configuration and available resources.

Offline attacks involve capturing the four-way handshake exchanged between a client device and the access point when the client connects to the Wi-Fi network.

The handshake contains cryptographic information necessary for deriving the PSK.

Attackers can capture this handshake through tools like Wireshark or aircrack-ng and then attempt to crack it using offline brute force or dictionary attacks.

Offline brute force attacks involve trying every possible combination of characters to find the correct PSK.

While this method can be effective, it is time-consuming and resource-intensive, especially for complex and lengthy passphrases.

To enhance security against brute force attacks, users are encouraged to use strong and unique passphrases.

Offline dictionary attacks, on the other hand, rely on a predefined list of commonly used words and phrases.

Attackers compare the captured handshake's cryptographic hash with entries in the dictionary.

If a match is found, the attacker has successfully discovered the PSK.

To protect against dictionary attacks, users should avoid using easily guessable words and phrases as passphrases.

WPA3's resistance to offline brute force and dictionary attacks is primarily due to its use of the Simultaneous Authentication of Equals (SAE) protocol.

SAE is a secure key exchange mechanism that thwarts attackers' efforts to capture and crack handshakes.

However, attackers can still attempt to compromise WPA3 by exploiting vulnerabilities in the implementation or configuration of Wi-Fi access points and clients.

For instance, weak or default passwords for device management interfaces can provide attackers with access to change network settings.

Once inside, attackers can manipulate network configurations or install rogue access points to intercept traffic.

To enhance the security of WPA3 networks, it is crucial to change default passwords and ensure strong access point security configurations.

Another potential avenue for attackers is the use of rogue Wi-Fi access points, which mimic legitimate networks and lure unsuspecting users to connect.

These rogue access points can capture login credentials, session cookies, and other sensitive information.

To mitigate this threat, users should exercise caution when connecting to Wi-Fi networks, especially in public places, and verify the legitimacy of the network.

Furthermore, attackers may exploit zero-day vulnerabilities in Wi-Fi chipsets or firmware, allowing them to bypass WPA3 encryption entirely.

Device manufacturers regularly release patches to address security vulnerabilities, making it essential for users to keep their Wi-Fi-enabled devices up to date.

The evolution of Wi-Fi security continues with advancements in encryption algorithms and protocols.

WPA3-SAE, with its robust key exchange mechanism, represents a significant improvement in wireless security.

However, it is essential to remain vigilant and proactive in defending against potential threats.

Security practitioners should regularly monitor for signs of unauthorized access, unusual network activity, or rogue access points.

Additionally, educating users about the importance of strong passphrases, default password changes, and network awareness can further bolster wireless network security.

In summary, while cracking WPA3 encryption presents challenges for attackers, it is not impossible.

Security professionals and users must remain informed about potential threats and best practices to protect their Wi-Fi networks effectively.

The ongoing battle between defenders and attackers in the realm of wireless network security underscores the need for continuous vigilance and adaptation to emerging threats and vulnerabilities.

Wireless Intrusion Detection and Prevention (WIDP) is a critical component of modern network security strategies, specifically tailored to protect wireless networks from various threats and vulnerabilities.

WIDP systems are designed to monitor wireless network traffic, detect suspicious or malicious activity, and take proactive measures to prevent unauthorized access or attacks.

Wireless networks, including Wi-Fi, have become integral to both personal and business environments, offering convenience and flexibility.

However, they also present unique security challenges due to their inherent characteristics, such as radio frequency signals that can extend beyond physical boundaries, making them susceptible to eavesdropping and unauthorized access.

As a result, organizations need robust WIDP solutions to safeguard their wireless networks.

WIDP systems employ a range of detection techniques to identify potential threats and vulnerabilities in wireless networks.

One common approach is signature-based detection, where the system compares network traffic against a database of known attack patterns and signatures.

When a match is found, the WIDP system generates an alert or takes preventive action.

Signature-based detection is effective against well-known and documented attacks.

However, it may struggle to detect zero-day or previously unknown threats.

To address this limitation, anomaly-based detection is another technique employed by WIDP systems.

Anomaly-based detection establishes a baseline of normal network behavior and identifies deviations from this baseline.

When the system detects unusual or suspicious activity, it triggers an alert or initiates preventive measures.

Anomaly-based detection is effective at identifying new and previously unknown threats.

However, it may also generate false positives if the baseline is not adequately defined or if legitimate network behavior changes.

Additionally, behavior-based detection analyzes the behavior of wireless clients and access points to detect deviations from expected norms.

This approach can identify malicious or compromised devices by monitoring their activities and communication patterns.

Behavior-based detection is particularly useful in identifying insider threats and compromised endpoints.

Another important aspect of WIDP is the prevention component, which goes beyond detection to actively block or mitigate threats.

WIDP systems can employ various prevention techniques, such as deauthentication, containment, or blocking unauthorized devices from accessing the network.

Deauthentication involves disconnecting unauthorized devices from the network, preventing further communication.

Containment isolates compromised devices to prevent lateral movement within the network.

Blocking prevents unauthorized devices from connecting to the network in the first place.

WIDP systems can also take automated actions based on predefined policies, such as blocking certain types of traffic or implementing access controls.

To effectively protect wireless networks, organizations should consider several best practices when implementing WIDP solutions.

Firstly, they should ensure comprehensive coverage by deploying WIDP sensors strategically throughout the network.

This includes coverage in both indoor and outdoor areas, as well as support for various wireless technologies, such as Wi-Fi and Bluetooth.

Regular updates and signature database maintenance are essential to keep the WIDP system current and capable of detecting emerging threats.

Organizations should also define clear policies and procedures for responding to alerts generated by the WIDP system.

This includes incident response plans and communication protocols to address detected threats promptly.

Furthermore, the integration of WIDP with other security systems, such as firewalls and SIEM (Security Information and Event Management) solutions, can enhance overall network security.

Regular training and awareness programs for network administrators and users are vital to ensure that everyone understands the importance of WIDP and how to respond to security incidents.

In summary, Wireless Intrusion Detection and Prevention is a critical element of modern network security, addressing the unique challenges posed by wireless networks.

WIDP systems employ a range of detection techniques, including signature-based, anomaly-based, and behavior-based approaches, to identify and respond to threats.

Preventive measures, such as deauthentication, containment, and blocking, complement detection capabilities.

Organizations should follow best practices in deploying, maintaining, and integrating WIDP solutions to safeguard their wireless networks effectively.

As wireless technology continues to evolve, so too must the strategies and technologies used to protect these networks from an ever-expanding array of threats and vulnerabilities.

Chapter 7: Auditing Cloud-Based Systems

Cloud Configuration Auditing and Hardening is a critical component of cloud security, aimed at ensuring that cloud resources and services are configured in a secure and compliant manner.

As organizations increasingly migrate their infrastructure and applications to the cloud, the need to properly configure and secure these resources becomes paramount.

Misconfigurations are a leading cause of cloud security incidents, making cloud configuration auditing and hardening a vital practice.

One of the fundamental principles of cloud security is the shared responsibility model, which defines the division of security responsibilities between cloud service providers (CSPs) and cloud customers.

CSPs are responsible for the security of the cloud infrastructure, including the physical data centers, networking, and hypervisors.

Customers, on the other hand, are responsible for securing their data, applications, and configurations within the cloud.

Cloud configuration auditing involves reviewing and assessing the settings, permissions, and configurations of cloud resources to identify vulnerabilities and deviations from security best practices.

This process aims to uncover misconfigurations that could expose sensitive data, allow unauthorized access, or create other security risks.

Common cloud configuration auditing tasks include reviewing access control lists (ACLs), identity and access management (IAM) policies, firewall rules, encryption settings, and storage configurations.

Automated cloud security tools can assist in this process by continuously monitoring configurations and comparing them against predefined security baselines.

By regularly auditing cloud configurations, organizations can proactively identify and rectify issues before they can be exploited by attackers.

A critical aspect of cloud configuration auditing is the establishment of security baselines and best practices that align with industry standards and regulatory requirements.

Organizations should create a set of documented security standards and guidelines for configuring cloud resources, taking into account factors such as data sensitivity, compliance requirements, and the principle of least privilege.

These standards serve as a foundation for secure configuration and provide clear guidance for cloud administrators.

Implementing role-based access control (RBAC) is a crucial aspect of cloud configuration hardening.

RBAC ensures that users and services have the minimum necessary permissions to perform their tasks, reducing the risk of unauthorized access or privilege escalation.

Cloud administrators should regularly review and update IAM policies and permissions to align with the principle of least privilege.

Additionally, organizations should implement strong authentication mechanisms, such as multi-factor authentication (MFA), to enhance access security.

Another important aspect of cloud configuration hardening is the proper configuration of network security groups (NSGs) and firewalls to control inbound and outbound traffic to cloud resources.

By limiting access to only necessary ports and protocols, organizations can reduce the attack surface and prevent unauthorized access.

Encryption plays a pivotal role in cloud security, and hardening efforts should include the use of encryption for data at rest and in transit.

Organizations should leverage CSP-provided encryption services or implement their own encryption solutions to protect sensitive data.

Regular key management and rotation practices should be established to ensure the ongoing security of encryption keys.

Cloud resources should be regularly patched and updated to address security vulnerabilities.

Patching not only applies to virtual machines but also to cloud-native services and containerized applications.

Organizations should establish patch management processes and automate the deployment of security updates.

In addition to automated tools, organizations should also conduct manual reviews of cloud configurations to identify and remediate security gaps that automated tools may miss.

These manual reviews may include analyzing logs and conducting penetration testing to uncover potential weaknesses.

Regular security training and awareness programs for cloud administrators and users are essential to ensure that security best practices are followed.

Security education should cover topics like secure configuration, identity and access management, encryption, and incident response.

Cloud configuration auditing and hardening is an ongoing process, and organizations should continuously monitor, assess, and adjust their configurations to adapt to evolving threats and compliance requirements.

Security professionals should stay informed about emerging cloud security threats and vulnerabilities to proactively protect cloud environments.

In summary, Cloud Configuration Auditing and Hardening is a critical aspect of cloud security, aiming to prevent security incidents resulting from misconfigurations.

This practice involves regular auditing of cloud resources, adherence to security baselines and best practices, RBAC implementation, network security controls, encryption, patch management, and ongoing monitoring.

With the growing adoption of cloud services, organizations must prioritize cloud configuration auditing and hardening to protect their data and infrastructure effectively.

Ensuring data privacy and compliance in the cloud is a paramount concern for organizations that handle sensitive data and must adhere to various regulatory requirements.

The cloud computing model, while offering numerous benefits, introduces unique challenges when it comes to safeguarding data and meeting compliance standards.

To address these challenges, organizations must implement robust strategies, policies, and technical controls that prioritize data privacy and compliance in the cloud environment.

Data privacy involves protecting the confidentiality, integrity, and availability of data, ensuring that only authorized individuals can access and use it.

In a cloud environment, data privacy is essential because data often traverses networks and is stored in remote data centers operated by third-party providers.

To protect data privacy in the cloud, organizations must implement encryption mechanisms to secure data both in transit and at rest.

Encryption ensures that data remains confidential even if unauthorized parties gain access to it.

Additionally, organizations should consider using tokenization and data masking techniques to further protect sensitive information.

Another critical aspect of data privacy is data classification and access control.

Organizations should classify their data based on its sensitivity and establish strict access controls to ensure that only authorized users can view or modify sensitive data.

Role-based access control (RBAC) is a valuable tool for managing access permissions efficiently.

Cloud providers typically offer identity and access management (IAM) services that enable organizations to define and enforce access policies based on roles and responsibilities. To maintain data privacy and compliance, organizations must also carefully consider the location of their cloud data storage. Data sovereignty laws may require that certain data must remain within specific geographic regions or jurisdictions. Organizations should select cloud providers that offer data center locations compliant with relevant regulations. Cloud providers often have tools and features that facilitate data residency compliance.

Data breaches can have severe consequences for data privacy and compliance.

Organizations should implement robust security measures to protect against unauthorized access and data breaches in the cloud.

This includes using firewalls, intrusion detection systems, and intrusion prevention systems to monitor and protect cloud resources.

Regular security assessments and penetration testing can help identify vulnerabilities and weaknesses in cloud infrastructure and applications.

Furthermore, organizations should establish an incident response plan specific to cloud environments to respond promptly to security incidents and data breaches.

Compliance in the cloud involves adhering to industry-specific regulations, international standards, and contractual agreements.

For example, organizations in healthcare must comply with the Health Insurance Portability and Accountability Act (HIPAA), while financial institutions must adhere to the Payment Card Industry Data Security Standard (PCI DSS).

These regulations impose requirements related to data security, access controls, auditing, and reporting.

To achieve compliance in the cloud, organizations should select cloud providers that offer compliance certifications relevant to their industry.

Additionally, organizations must ensure that their cloud configurations and practices align with the specific requirements of the regulations they are subject to.

This may involve configuring encryption settings, access controls, and auditing capabilities to meet compliance standards.

Many cloud providers offer compliance documentation and tools to assist organizations in achieving and maintaining compliance.

Auditing and monitoring are fundamental for ensuring data privacy and compliance in the cloud.

Organizations should implement continuous monitoring and auditing solutions that track user activities, data access, and changes to cloud configurations.

These solutions can help detect unauthorized access or data breaches and provide the necessary audit trail for compliance reporting.

Organizations should also regularly review and assess their cloud configurations to identify and remediate any potential security or compliance gaps.

Automation plays a crucial role in maintaining data privacy and compliance in the cloud.

Automated security and compliance checks can help organizations ensure that their cloud resources continuously meet established standards and policies.

Many cloud providers offer tools and services that enable automated compliance assessments and remediation.

It's important to note that compliance is an ongoing process, not a one-time effort.

Organizations must stay informed about changes in regulations and standards that may affect their cloud environments.

Regular training and awareness programs for cloud administrators and users are essential to ensure that everyone understands their roles in maintaining data privacy and compliance.

Furthermore, organizations should conduct regular compliance audits and assessments to verify that their cloud environment continues to meet regulatory requirements.

In summary, ensuring data privacy and compliance in the cloud is a complex but essential undertaking for organizations.

It involves protecting sensitive data, implementing access controls, complying with industry-specific regulations, and conducting regular audits and assessments.

By following best practices, leveraging cloud provider tools, and staying vigilant, organizations can maintain data privacy and compliance in their cloud environments, mitigating risks and ensuring the security of their data and operations.

Chapter 8: Insider Threat Identification and Mitigation

Detecting insider threat behaviors and anomalies is a critical aspect of an organization's cybersecurity strategy, aimed at identifying and mitigating risks posed by employees, contractors, or other individuals with privileged access to the organization's systems and data.

Insider threats can encompass a wide range of malicious activities, from data theft and fraud to espionage and sabotage, making their detection and prevention a top priority.

One of the key challenges in detecting insider threats is distinguishing between normal user activities and those that indicate malicious intent.

Insiders often have legitimate access to systems and data, making it essential to identify deviations from established patterns or behaviors that may indicate suspicious activity.

To address this challenge, organizations deploy various technologies and strategies designed to detect insider threat behaviors and anomalies effectively.

User and entity behavior analytics (UEBA) is a prominent approach used in detecting insider threats.

UEBA solutions leverage machine learning and advanced analytics to establish a baseline of normal behavior for users and entities within an organization.

This baseline considers factors such as login times, locations, data access patterns, and typical work hours.

Once established, the UEBA system continuously monitors user and entity activities, comparing them to the baseline.

Deviations from the baseline, such as unusual data access or atypical login locations, trigger alerts that can prompt further investigation.

Insider threat detection is not limited to monitoring user activities alone; it also includes analyzing network traffic and data flows.

Anomalies in network traffic, such as unusually large data transfers or unexpected data access patterns, can be indicative of insider threats.

Therefore, network monitoring and analysis tools are essential components of a comprehensive insider threat detection strategy.

Another important aspect of detecting insider threats is the analysis of access logs and audit trails.

Organizations should maintain detailed logs of user activities, data access, and system events.

By regularly reviewing and analyzing these logs, security teams can identify patterns or actions that may indicate insider threats, such as repeated login failures, unauthorized access attempts, or suspicious file deletions.

Behavioral profiling is a technique used to identify insider threat behaviors.

It involves creating profiles of individual users or entities based on their typical behavior and comparing their current activities to these profiles.

For example, if a user who typically accesses certain data or systems suddenly starts accessing sensitive information unrelated to their job role, it may raise suspicion.

Another approach to detecting insider threats is the use of threat intelligence feeds and indicators of compromise (IoCs).

These feeds provide information about known threat actors, malicious IP addresses, and attack techniques.

By comparing network traffic and user activities to known IoCs, organizations can identify potential insider threat behaviors that match known attack patterns.

Behavioral analysis also extends to email and communication platforms, where insiders may use these channels to exfiltrate data or communicate with malicious actors.

Monitoring email content and communication patterns can help detect insider threat behaviors, such as sending sensitive data to external recipients or using unusual language indicative of malicious intent.

Endpoint detection and response (EDR) solutions play a vital role in detecting insider threats on individual devices.

EDR solutions monitor endpoints for signs of suspicious activity, such as file changes, process execution, and registry modifications.

They can identify insider threat behaviors such as unauthorized data transfers, privilege escalation attempts, or the installation of unauthorized software.

Data loss prevention (DLP) solutions are essential tools in detecting insider threats involving data exfiltration.

DLP solutions monitor and control the movement of sensitive data within and outside the organization.

They can detect insider threat behaviors like copying sensitive files to external storage devices, uploading sensitive data to cloud services, or sending it via email.

Human factors also play a significant role in detecting insider threats.

Security awareness training and a culture of vigilance within the organization can encourage employees to report suspicious activities or insider threat behaviors they observe.

Whistleblower programs and clear reporting mechanisms can provide employees with a safe way to raise concerns about potential insider threats.

Additionally, threat hunting is a proactive approach to insider threat detection.

Security teams actively seek out signs of insider threats by analyzing historical data, conducting deep dives into user and entity behaviors, and investigating anomalies that may not trigger automated alerts.

This human-driven approach can uncover subtle insider threat behaviors that automated systems may overlook.

In summary, detecting insider threat behaviors and anomalies is a multifaceted endeavor that involves a combination of technology, behavioral analysis, and human vigilance.

Organizations must leverage a range of tools and strategies to effectively identify potential insider threats.

By implementing advanced monitoring and analysis techniques, organizations can enhance their ability to detect and respond to insider threat behaviors, reducing the risk of insider-related incidents and protecting sensitive data and assets. Mitigating insider threat risks is a crucial component of an organization's overall cybersecurity strategy, as insider threats pose significant dangers to the confidentiality, integrity, and availability of sensitive data and systems.

These threats can arise from employees, contractors, vendors, or anyone with authorized access to an organization's resources, making it essential to implement effective strategies for prevention and mitigation.

One of the fundamental strategies for mitigating insider threats is to establish a robust security culture within the organization. This culture should emphasize the importance of security, privacy, and ethical behavior and should be communicated throughout the organization from top management down. Employees at all levels should understand their role in safeguarding sensitive data and systems, and they should be encouraged to report any suspicious activity or potential insider threats promptly.

An essential aspect of creating a security culture is providing comprehensive security awareness training to all employees. Training programs should cover topics such as recognizing phishing attempts, safe data handling practices, the importance of strong passwords, and the consequences of insider threats.

By educating employees about security best practices, organizations can empower them to make informed decisions and act as a first line of defense against insider threats.

Another critical strategy is implementing robust access controls and user permissions.

Organizations should employ the principle of least privilege (PoLP), ensuring that users have access only to the resources and data necessary for their specific job roles.

This limits the potential damage an insider can inflict, as they won't have unrestricted access to sensitive information or systems.

Regularly reviewing and updating user permissions is essential, as employees' roles and responsibilities may change over time.

Implementing strong authentication mechanisms is also crucial in mitigating insider threat risks.

Multi-factor authentication (MFA) should be enforced for accessing sensitive systems and data.

MFA adds an extra layer of security by requiring users to provide multiple forms of verification, such as something they know (password) and something they have (a token or smartphone).

Monitoring and auditing user activities and data access is an integral part of insider threat mitigation.

Organizations should implement robust logging mechanisms that capture user actions, system events, and data access.

These logs should be regularly reviewed for any anomalies or suspicious activities. Intrusion detection systems (IDS) and intrusion prevention systems (IPS) can help identify and respond to insider threat behaviors in real-time.

Network traffic analysis tools can also aid in detecting unauthorized data transfers or unusual data access patterns.

Employee monitoring and behavior analysis are essential components of insider threat mitigation.

While monitoring, organizations should respect privacy and legal considerations, ensuring that employee rights are protected. Insider threat detection solutions, such as user and entity behavior analytics (UEBA) systems, use machine learning algorithms to analyze user behavior and identify deviations from normal patterns.

These solutions can help detect insider threat behaviors that may not be immediately apparent through manual analysis.

Incident response plans specific to insider threats should be developed and regularly tested.

These plans should outline the steps to be taken when insider threats are detected, including immediate containment, investigation, and legal actions if necessary.

A critical element of an insider threat incident response plan is communication.

The plan should define the reporting chain, detailing whom to notify when insider threats are suspected or confirmed.

Organizations should also establish relationships with law enforcement agencies and legal counsel to ensure a coordinated response to insider threat incidents.

Whistleblower programs can provide employees with a secure and anonymous channel for reporting insider threats or unethical behavior.

These programs should be promoted and communicated within the organization to encourage employees to come forward with concerns.

In addition to technology-based solutions, organizations can also employ psychological profiling and early intervention strategies.

Psychological profiling involves identifying employees who may be at risk of becoming insider threats based on their behavior, attitudes, or personal circumstances.

Early intervention strategies aim to provide support and assistance to employees who may be experiencing personal or professional challenges that could lead to insider threats.

Offering counseling services, mentoring, and career development opportunities can help address the underlying causes of potential insider threat behaviors.

Organizations should conduct regular security assessments and penetration tests to identify vulnerabilities in their systems and networks that could be exploited by insiders.

These assessments should also include social engineering tests to evaluate employees' susceptibility to manipulation by malicious insiders.

Finally, collaboration with other organizations and sharing threat intelligence can enhance insider threat mitigation efforts.

Participating in industry-specific information sharing and analysis centers (ISACs) and collaborating with peer organizations can provide valuable insights into emerging insider threat trends and tactics.

In summary, mitigating insider threat risks requires a multifaceted approach that combines technology, training, culture, and proactive monitoring.

By implementing robust security measures, fostering a security-conscious culture, and being vigilant in detecting and responding to insider threat behaviors, organizations can significantly reduce the risks posed by insiders with malicious intent.

Chapter 9: Compliance and Regulatory Auditing

Navigating security standards and frameworks is an essential aspect of developing a robust and effective cybersecurity program for organizations of all sizes and industries.

These standards and frameworks serve as critical guides and reference points to help organizations establish and maintain a strong security posture.

They provide a structured approach to addressing security concerns and aligning security practices with industry best practices and regulatory requirements.

One of the most widely recognized and adopted security frameworks is the NIST Cybersecurity Framework, published by the National Institute of Standards and Technology (NIST).

The NIST Cybersecurity Framework offers a comprehensive set of guidelines, best practices, and controls to help organizations manage and reduce cybersecurity risks.

It consists of five core functions: Identify, Protect, Detect, Respond, and Recover, which guide organizations in understanding their cybersecurity risks, protecting against threats, detecting incidents, responding to and recovering from security breaches.

The NIST Cybersecurity Framework is widely used in the United States and has gained international recognition as a valuable resource for improving cybersecurity.

Another prominent framework is ISO/IEC 27001, which sets the standards for establishing, implementing, maintaining, and continually improving an information security management system (ISMS).

ISO/IEC 27001 is known for its rigorous approach to information security and provides a systematic way to identify, assess, and mitigate security risks.

Organizations seeking ISO/IEC 27001 certification must adhere to a set of controls and practices to ensure the confidentiality, integrity, and availability of sensitive information.

The Payment Card Industry Data Security Standard (PCI DSS) is another widely adopted framework, particularly in the payment card industry.

PCI DSS provides specific requirements for securing credit card data during transactions, storage, and processing.

Organizations that handle credit card information must comply with PCI DSS to protect cardholder data from breaches and fraud.

For federal agencies and organizations that deal with sensitive government information, the Federal Risk and Authorization Management Program (FedRAMP) provides a standardized approach to security assessment, authorization, and continuous monitoring.

FedRAMP ensures that cloud service providers (CSPs) meet rigorous security standards when offering services to the federal government.

Another crucial framework is the Center for Internet Security (CIS) Controls, formerly known as the SANS Top 20 Critical Security Controls.

These controls provide a prioritized set of actions that organizations can take to improve their cybersecurity posture.

They cover a broad range of security areas, including asset management, vulnerability assessment, secure configuration, and incident response.

Many organizations find the CIS Controls valuable in focusing their security efforts on the most critical and impactful areas.

The Health Insurance Portability and Accountability Act (HIPAA) Security Rule is essential for healthcare organizations that handle protected health information (PHI).

HIPAA sets security standards and requirements for safeguarding PHI to ensure the privacy and security of patients' health information.

Compliance with HIPAA is mandatory for healthcare providers, health plans, and healthcare clearinghouses.

The General Data Protection Regulation (GDPR) is a European Union (EU) regulation that governs the protection of personal data of EU citizens.

Although not a framework in the traditional sense, GDPR mandates strict data protection measures, data subject rights, and breach notification requirements for organizations that process EU personal data.

Frameworks like the CIS Controls, NIST Cybersecurity Framework, and ISO/IEC 27001 are flexible and adaptable, allowing organizations to tailor their security programs to their specific needs and risk profiles.

One of the critical challenges organizations face when navigating security standards and frameworks is determining which ones are most relevant to their operations and compliance requirements.

This requires a thorough assessment of the organization's industry, regulatory environment, and business objectives.

It is essential to identify the specific security standards and frameworks that align with these factors and address the organization's unique security risks.

Once identified, organizations can develop a roadmap for implementing the selected standards and frameworks.

This roadmap should include a detailed plan for assessing current security practices, identifying gaps, and implementing necessary controls and processes.

Organizations should also establish clear ownership and accountability for security initiatives, ensuring that responsible individuals or teams are designated to oversee compliance efforts. Regular risk assessments and security audits are essential components of navigating security standards and frameworks effectively.

These assessments help organizations evaluate their security posture, identify vulnerabilities, and measure progress toward compliance and risk reduction goals.

External audits and assessments may also be required to demonstrate compliance with specific standards or regulations. Organizations should maintain documentation of their security practices, policies, and procedures to support compliance efforts. This documentation serves as evidence of adherence to security standards and frameworks and can be invaluable during audits and assessments.

Many organizations also leverage cybersecurity frameworks to guide incident response planning and preparation.

Frameworks like the NIST Cybersecurity Framework and CIS Controls offer valuable guidance on developing incident response plans, including identifying roles and responsibilities, establishing communication protocols, and conducting post-incident analysis.

Regular training and awareness programs are essential for ensuring that employees understand and adhere to the security standards and frameworks relevant to their roles.

Employees should be educated on the importance of security practices, data protection, and compliance requirements.

Ultimately, navigating security standards and frameworks is an ongoing and evolving process.

As the threat landscape and regulatory environment continue to change, organizations must stay informed and adapt their security programs accordingly.

Regularly reviewing and updating security policies and controls is essential for maintaining compliance and effectively mitigating cybersecurity risks.

By embracing a proactive and strategic approach to security standards and frameworks, organizations can enhance their cybersecurity posture, protect sensitive data, and mitigate potential threats effectively.

Achieving compliance with data protection regulations is a critical objective for organizations that handle personal data in today's digital age.

These regulations are designed to safeguard the privacy and rights of individuals, ensuring that their personal information is collected, processed, and stored responsibly and securely.

One of the most well-known data protection regulations globally is the General Data Protection Regulation (GDPR), enacted by the European Union (EU).

GDPR sets a high standard for data protection, and it applies not only to EU-based organizations but also to any organization that processes personal data of EU citizens.

Compliance with GDPR requires organizations to implement strict data protection measures, appoint data protection officers (DPOs), and report data breaches within specified timeframes.

Another significant data protection regulation is the California Consumer Privacy Act (CCPA), which applies to businesses operating in California and handling the personal information of California residents.

CCPA grants consumers certain rights, including the right to know what personal information is being collected and the right to opt-out of the sale of their data.

To achieve compliance with data protection regulations like GDPR and CCPA, organizations must first assess their data processing activities.

This assessment involves identifying all data flows within the organization, including data collection, storage, sharing, and processing.

Once data flows are mapped, organizations can categorize the data they handle, distinguishing between personal data and other types of data.

Personal data is any information that can directly or indirectly identify an individual, such as names, email addresses, phone numbers, and even IP addresses.

Having categorized personal data, organizations can then implement data protection measures, including encryption, access controls, and regular data protection impact assessments (DPIAs).

DPIAs help organizations identify and mitigate privacy risks associated with their data processing activities.

To ensure compliance, organizations should appoint a data protection officer (DPO) if required by the applicable regulations.

A DPO is responsible for overseeing data protection efforts within the organization, acting as a point of contact for data subjects, and ensuring that the organization complies with data protection regulations.

Implementing robust security measures is a crucial aspect of achieving compliance with data protection regulations.

Encryption, for example, ensures that personal data remains confidential and protected from unauthorized access.

Access controls limit who can access and process personal data, reducing the risk of data breaches.

Regular security assessments and penetration testing can help identify vulnerabilities and weaknesses in the organization's data protection measures.

Data protection regulations often require organizations to appoint a privacy officer responsible for managing privacy compliance efforts.

The privacy officer ensures that the organization complies with data protection regulations, develops privacy policies and procedures, and educates employees about privacy best practices.

Privacy policies are essential documents that outline how an organization collects, processes, stores, and shares personal data.

These policies should be transparent, easy to understand, and easily accessible to data subjects.

To achieve compliance, organizations must obtain the explicit consent of data subjects before collecting and processing their personal data.

Consent forms should clearly state the purpose of data collection and processing and provide an option for data subjects to withdraw their consent at any time.

Data subjects also have the right to access their personal data held by organizations.

To comply with this requirement, organizations must establish procedures for data subjects to request access to their data and provide the requested information within specified timeframes.

Data subjects can also request the deletion or correction of their personal data under certain circumstances.

Organizations must have processes in place to address these requests promptly.

One of the most challenging aspects of achieving compliance with data protection regulations is reporting data breaches.

Data breaches can occur due to various factors, including cyberattacks, human error, or technical failures.

Organizations must have an incident response plan that outlines how to detect, respond to, and report data breaches.

In many cases, organizations must report data breaches to regulatory authorities and affected data subjects within specific timeframes.

Achieving compliance with data protection regulations is an ongoing process that requires continuous monitoring and adaptation.

Regulations may change or evolve, and organizations must stay up-to-date with these changes to ensure ongoing compliance.

Regular audits and assessments of data protection practices can help organizations identify areas for improvement and ensure that they remain in compliance with data protection regulations.

Compliance with data protection regulations not only helps organizations avoid legal consequences but also builds trust with customers and demonstrates a commitment to protecting their privacy.

Customers are more likely to trust organizations that handle their data responsibly and transparently.

In summary, achieving compliance with data protection regulations is a complex but essential task for organizations in today's data-driven world.

By assessing data processing activities, implementing security measures, appointing DPOs and privacy officers, obtaining consent, and developing transparent privacy policies, organizations can navigate the intricate landscape of data protection regulations successfully.

Moreover, organizations must have robust incident response plans in place to report and mitigate data breaches promptly.

Staying informed about changes in regulations and regularly auditing data protection practices ensures ongoing compliance and helps build trust with customers.

Chapter 10: Advanced Ethical Hacking Case Studies

Real-world ethical hacking success stories provide invaluable insights into the practical application of ethical hacking techniques and the positive impact they can have on organizations.

These stories showcase the accomplishments of ethical hackers, also known as white hat hackers, who use their skills to identify and remediate vulnerabilities before malicious actors can exploit them.

One such success story involves a financial institution that hired an ethical hacking team to assess the security of its online banking platform.

The ethical hackers discovered a critical vulnerability that could have allowed attackers to steal sensitive customer data and conduct fraudulent transactions.

By promptly addressing the vulnerability, the financial institution prevented a potential security breach and protected its customers from financial harm.

Another remarkable success story comes from a healthcare organization that enlisted ethical hackers to evaluate the security of its electronic health records (EHR) system.

During the assessment, the ethical hackers identified vulnerabilities that could have exposed patients' medical records to unauthorized access.

By addressing these vulnerabilities and enhancing their security measures, the healthcare organization ensured the confidentiality and integrity of patient data.

Ethical hacking has also played a crucial role in safeguarding critical infrastructure. In one case, a power grid operator hired ethical hackers to assess the security of its control systems.

The ethical hackers identified vulnerabilities that could have been exploited to disrupt electricity distribution, potentially causing widespread outages.

The power grid operator promptly implemented security improvements based on the ethical hackers' findings, enhancing the resilience of the energy infrastructure.

Ethical hacking success stories extend to the realm of e-commerce, where businesses rely on secure online platforms for transactions.

An e-commerce company engaged ethical hackers to perform penetration testing on its website and mobile applications.

During the assessment, the ethical hackers identified a vulnerability in the payment processing system that could have exposed customer payment data.

By swiftly addressing the issue and improving security measures, the e-commerce company protected its customers from potential financial losses and data breaches.

The finance industry has seen numerous ethical hacking successes, including a global bank that sought to enhance the security of its ATM network.

Ethical hackers conducted a thorough assessment and discovered vulnerabilities that could have allowed cybercriminals to compromise ATM machines and steal cash.

By addressing these vulnerabilities, the bank ensured the integrity of its ATM network and the security of customers' funds.

In the world of telecommunications, ethical hackers have played a pivotal role in identifying and mitigating vulnerabilities in mobile networks.

A mobile service provider engaged ethical hackers to assess its network infrastructure, and they uncovered vulnerabilities that could have been exploited for eavesdropping and unauthorized access.

The provider promptly implemented security measures to protect the privacy and security of its subscribers.

Ethical hacking success stories also extend to software development, with a software company benefiting from the expertise of ethical hackers.

During a security assessment of their flagship software product, the ethical hackers discovered a critical vulnerability that could have allowed remote code execution.

By swiftly patching the vulnerability and conducting a comprehensive security review, the software company prevented potential security incidents and protected its customers' data.

In the realm of cloud computing, an organization leveraging cloud services enlisted ethical hackers to assess the security of its cloud infrastructure.

The ethical hackers identified configuration weaknesses that could have exposed sensitive data stored in the cloud to unauthorized access.

By addressing these issues and implementing stronger access controls, the organization secured its cloud-based assets and data.

Ethical hacking success stories also highlight the importance of proactive security measures. In one instance, a technology company conducted a red team exercise led by ethical hackers.

During the exercise, the ethical hackers successfully simulated a cyberattack, exposing vulnerabilities in the organization's defenses.

The company used the insights gained from the exercise to enhance its security posture and better prepare for real-world threats.

Ethical hackers have even contributed to the protection of national security. Government agencies have engaged ethical hackers to assess the security of critical systems and infrastructure.

In one case, ethical hackers identified vulnerabilities in a government agency's network that could have been exploited to gain unauthorized access to sensitive information.

By remediating these vulnerabilities, the agency bolstered its cybersecurity defenses and safeguarded national security interests.

These real-world ethical hacking success stories demonstrate the significance of proactive security assessments and the positive impact of ethical hackers on organizations of all types.

By identifying vulnerabilities and weaknesses before malicious actors can exploit them, ethical hackers help protect data, finances, critical infrastructure, and even national security.

Organizations that prioritize security assessments and collaborate with ethical hackers can significantly enhance their cybersecurity posture and mitigate potential risks.

Analyzing complex security breaches and their subsequent remediations is an essential aspect of strengthening an organization's cybersecurity posture.

Complex security breaches often involve multiple layers of compromise and require meticulous investigation to uncover the full extent of the damage.

These breaches can have severe consequences, including data theft, financial losses, reputational damage, and legal liabilities.

One of the first steps in analyzing a complex security breach is to gather as much information as possible about the incident.

This includes collecting logs, network traffic data, and any available evidence of the breach's origin and progression.

Understanding the initial entry point used by attackers is crucial, as it can help organizations identify and remediate vulnerabilities.

In many cases, complex security breaches start with a seemingly innocuous event, such as a phishing email or a compromised user account.

Once inside the network, attackers often move laterally to gain access to critical systems and sensitive data.

To analyze these breaches effectively, organizations must have skilled incident response teams in place.

These teams are responsible for coordinating the investigation, containing the breach, and minimizing further damage.

The incident response process begins with identifying the affected systems and isolating them from the rest of the network to prevent the spread of the breach.

Simultaneously, digital forensics experts collect and analyze evidence to determine the attackers' methods and objectives.

Analyzing complex security breaches often involves reverse engineering malware and examining the tactics, techniques, and procedures (TTPs) used by the attackers.

Once the breach's scope and methodology are understood, organizations can develop a remediation plan.

This plan typically involves patching vulnerabilities, removing malware, and implementing stronger security controls.

In some cases, organizations may decide to rebuild compromised systems from scratch to ensure their integrity.

During the remediation phase, it's essential to address the root causes of the breach, which may include weak passwords, unpatched software, or inadequate access controls.

Complex security breaches often reveal weaknesses in an organization's security posture that must be addressed to prevent future incidents.

Communication is a critical component of analyzing and remediating complex security breaches.

Organizations must promptly inform affected parties, including customers, employees, and regulatory authorities, about the breach and its impact.

Transparency builds trust and helps organizations manage the fallout from the incident.

Furthermore, organizations must work closely with law enforcement agencies when necessary, as cyberattacks may involve criminal activity.

Analyzing complex security breaches requires a multi-disciplinary approach that involves IT, cybersecurity, legal, and public relations teams.

These teams must collaborate to manage the incident effectively and ensure a coordinated response.

The post-incident analysis also extends to evaluating the effectiveness of the organization's incident response plan.

Identifying areas for improvement and refining the plan is crucial to enhancing an organization's resilience against future breaches.

Complex security breaches often involve advanced persistent threats (APTs), which are well-funded and highly motivated adversaries.

APTs are known for their patience and persistence, which makes them challenging to detect and mitigate.

To defend against APTs, organizations must adopt proactive security measures, such as threat hunting and continuous monitoring.

Threat hunting involves actively searching for signs of compromise within the network, even when no alarms or alerts have been triggered.

This proactive approach can help detect APTs early in their lifecycle, reducing the potential impact of a breach.

Continuous monitoring involves real-time analysis of network traffic and behavior to identify unusual or suspicious activity.

This can help organizations spot indicators of compromise and take swift action to contain and remediate the breach.

Complex security breaches often result in significant financial costs for organizations.

These costs may include expenses related to incident response, legal fees, regulatory fines, and costs associated with notifying affected parties and providing credit monitoring services.

Moreover, the long-term reputational damage caused by a security breach can lead to a loss of customers and revenue.

To mitigate these financial risks, organizations must invest in robust cybersecurity measures and insurance policies that cover the costs of a breach.

In summary, analyzing complex security breaches and their remediations is a critical process for organizations in today's digital landscape.

These breaches are becoming increasingly sophisticated, and their consequences can be severe.

By promptly and effectively responding to complex security breaches, organizations can minimize the damage, protect their assets and reputation, and enhance their overall cybersecurity posture.

Continuous improvement and proactive security measures are essential to defend against advanced persistent threats and other adversaries in the evolving threat landscape.

BOOK 4
SECURITY AUDITING MASTERY
ADVANCED INSIGHTS FOR ETHICAL HACKERS

ROB BOTWRIGHT

Chapter 1: The Ethical Hacker's Journey

The evolution of ethical hacking has been a dynamic and transformative journey that mirrors the rapid advancements in information technology and cybersecurity.

Ethical hacking, also known as white hat hacking or penetration testing, is the practice of intentionally probing computer systems, networks, and applications to identify vulnerabilities and weaknesses before malicious hackers can exploit them.

To understand its evolution, it's crucial to delve into its origins, development, and its role in the contemporary cybersecurity landscape.

The roots of ethical hacking can be traced back to the early days of computing when computer enthusiasts and hobbyists discovered vulnerabilities in computer systems for educational purposes.

These early hackers, known as "phone phreaks," explored the inner workings of telephone systems and computer networks in the 1970s.

Their activities laid the foundation for ethical hacking by highlighting the need for security testing and vulnerability assessment.

In the 1980s, as the internet began to emerge, ethical hacking started to take shape as a distinct discipline.

Security experts and organizations recognized the necessity of assessing network security to protect sensitive data and critical infrastructure.

As a result, ethical hackers began conducting controlled assessments and tests to identify vulnerabilities, providing valuable insights into the security of computer systems.

One of the landmark events in the evolution of ethical hacking was the founding of the first computer security conference, DEFCON, in 1993.

DEFCON brought together security professionals, hackers, and enthusiasts to share knowledge, discuss emerging threats, and showcase their skills.

This gathering played a pivotal role in fostering the ethical hacking community and promoting responsible hacking practices.

The late 1990s saw the formalization of ethical hacking as a legitimate and recognized profession.

Organizations began hiring certified ethical hackers to conduct security assessments, penetration tests, and vulnerability scans.

To meet the growing demand for skilled professionals, certification programs like Certified Ethical Hacker (CEH) were introduced, providing individuals with a structured path to becoming ethical hackers.

The early 2000s marked a significant shift in the role of ethical hackers as cyber threats became more sophisticated and widespread.

The rise of malware, cyberattacks, and data breaches emphasized the critical need for robust cybersecurity measures.

Ethical hackers began playing a crucial role in not only identifying vulnerabilities but also assisting organizations in remediation and improving their security posture.

In response to evolving threats, ethical hackers expanded their skill sets beyond network and system vulnerabilities to include web application security, mobile device security, and cloud computing security.

The emergence of bug bounty programs, where organizations reward ethical hackers for responsibly disclosing vulnerabilities, further encouraged collaboration between hackers and the companies they tested.

Bug bounty programs became an essential tool for organizations to crowdsource security testing and identify vulnerabilities quickly.

Today, ethical hacking has become an integral part of the cybersecurity ecosystem.

Organizations across various industries rely on ethical hackers to assess their defenses, identify weaknesses, and help protect against cyber threats.

The ethical hacking community has grown exponentially, with professionals continuously sharing knowledge, research, and best practices to stay ahead of emerging threats.

Furthermore, ethical hacking has branched into specialized areas, including penetration testing, red teaming, and incident response, reflecting the multifaceted nature of modern cybersecurity challenges.

Ethical hacking is no longer limited to the realm of IT security; it encompasses a broader scope that includes industrial control systems (ICS), IoT devices, and critical infrastructure protection.

As technology continues to advance, ethical hackers face new challenges in securing emerging technologies such as artificial intelligence (AI), blockchain, and quantum computing.

The future of ethical hacking will undoubtedly involve adapting to these evolving technologies and developing innovative techniques to assess their security.

Additionally, ethical hacking will play a critical role in addressing global cybersecurity challenges, such as defending against nation-state-sponsored cyberattacks and protecting critical infrastructure from digital threats.

The ethical hacking profession will continue to evolve and expand, with ethical hackers serving as cybersecurity guardians, helping organizations navigate the ever-changing threat landscape.

In summary, the evolution of ethical hacking has been marked by its transformation from a niche hobby to a vital profession in safeguarding the digital world.

Ethical hackers have played a pivotal role in identifying vulnerabilities, promoting responsible hacking practices, and helping organizations defend against cyber threats.

As technology advances, ethical hacking will remain at the forefront of cybersecurity, ensuring the continued security and resilience of the digital age.

Building ethical hacking skills and cultivating the right mindset is a journey that requires dedication, continuous learning, and a strong commitment to ethical principles.

Ethical hacking is not just about technical expertise but also about having the curiosity and determination to uncover vulnerabilities and secure digital environments.

One of the fundamental building blocks for aspiring ethical hackers is a solid understanding of computer networks and operating systems.

You should be familiar with how data travels across networks, the role of protocols, and the architecture of operating systems.

Knowledge of programming languages such as Python, C++, and scripting languages like PowerShell can be invaluable for automating tasks and developing custom tools for hacking simulations.

Equally important is a comprehensive understanding of cybersecurity concepts, including encryption, authentication, access control, and risk assessment.

Building ethical hacking skills often begins with setting up a safe and controlled lab environment where you can practice without causing harm.

This lab environment should mimic real-world systems and networks, allowing you to experiment, make mistakes, and learn from them.

You can set up virtual labs using software like VirtualBox, VMware, or cloud-based services like Amazon Web Services (AWS) and Microsoft Azure.

In your lab, you can create various virtual machines (VMs) to simulate different operating systems and network configurations.

Hands-on experience is crucial in ethical hacking, as it enables you to develop practical skills in identifying vulnerabilities, exploiting them, and securing systems.

A key aspect of ethical hacking is learning how to conduct reconnaissance and information gathering, which involves gathering as much data as possible about a target.

This information can include IP addresses, domain names, email addresses, and publicly available information about the target organization.

Ethical hackers often use open-source intelligence (OSINT) techniques to collect this data from publicly accessible sources like websites, social media, and online databases.

Learning how to use OSINT tools and techniques is an essential skill for an ethical hacker.

Next, ethical hackers must delve into the world of vulnerability assessment and penetration testing.

Vulnerability assessment involves scanning systems and networks to identify known vulnerabilities, such as unpatched software or misconfigured settings.

Penetration testing, on the other hand, goes a step further by attempting to exploit these vulnerabilities to gain unauthorized access.

Tools like Nessus, OpenVAS, and Metasploit are commonly used in the vulnerability assessment and penetration testing processes.

It's crucial to conduct penetration tests ethically, with proper authorization and within the bounds of legal and ethical guidelines.

A vital aspect of ethical hacking is understanding the importance of ethics and legality.

Ethical hackers must always operate within the boundaries of the law and follow strict ethical guidelines.

Unauthorized hacking or any malicious activity is not only unethical but also illegal and can lead to severe consequences.

Therefore, aspiring ethical hackers should familiarize themselves with relevant laws, regulations, and ethical codes, such as the Certified Ethical Hacker (CEH) Code of Ethics.

Building a strong ethical hacking mindset involves adopting the mindset of a hacker while adhering to ethical principles.

This mindset entails thinking critically, being resourceful, and having a relentless curiosity to uncover vulnerabilities and weaknesses.

It also involves a commitment to the ethical use of hacking skills for the greater good of organizations and society.

To further develop your ethical hacking skills and mindset, consider pursuing formal education and certifications in cybersecurity and ethical hacking.

Certifications like Certified Ethical Hacker (CEH), CompTIA Security+, and Certified Information Systems Security Professional (CISSP) can provide valuable knowledge and recognition in the field.

Networking and collaboration with other cybersecurity professionals and ethical hackers can also be instrumental in your growth.

Engage in online forums, attend cybersecurity conferences, and join local cybersecurity groups to stay updated on the latest trends and exchange knowledge with peers.

Additionally, staying informed about emerging threats, vulnerabilities, and hacking techniques is crucial in the ever-evolving field of ethical hacking.

Subscribe to cybersecurity news sources, follow security researchers on social media, and participate in capture the flag (CTF) competitions to sharpen your skills.

Developing a strong foundation in ethical hacking also requires mastering various tools and frameworks commonly used in the field.

These tools include Wireshark for network analysis, Burp Suite for web application testing, and Nmap for network scanning.

Knowledge of Linux is essential, as many hacking tools and scripts are designed for this operating system.

In addition to technical skills, ethical hackers should cultivate excellent communication skills.

The ability to document findings, write reports, and communicate effectively with technical and non-technical stakeholders is crucial in the ethical hacking process.

Ethical hackers often work closely with organizations' IT and security teams to remediate vulnerabilities and enhance security.

Finally, building ethical hacking skills and mindset is an ongoing process.

Technology and cyber threats continually evolve, requiring ethical hackers to adapt, learn, and stay one step ahead of adversaries.

Continuous learning and professional development are key to thriving in the dynamic field of ethical hacking.

In summary, building ethical hacking skills and mindset is a journey that combines technical expertise, ethical principles, and a relentless curiosity to uncover vulnerabilities and enhance cybersecurity.

It involves hands-on experience, ethical guidelines, legal awareness, and ongoing learning to stay at the forefront of the field.

Aspiring ethical hackers should embrace the challenge, commit to ethical practices, and strive to make the digital world more secure for all.

Chapter 2: Advanced Audit Methodologies

Comprehensive security assessment frameworks play a pivotal role in evaluating the security posture of organizations, helping them identify vulnerabilities and weaknesses in their systems, networks, and applications.

These frameworks provide structured methodologies and guidelines for conducting thorough security assessments, ensuring that no critical aspect of security is overlooked.

One of the most widely recognized and adopted security assessment frameworks is the National Institute of Standards and Technology (NIST) Cybersecurity Framework.

This framework was developed by NIST to help organizations across various sectors manage and improve their cybersecurity practices.

It consists of a set of core functions – Identify, Protect, Detect, Respond, and Recover – which guide organizations in assessing their current cybersecurity measures and developing strategies for improvement.

The NIST Cybersecurity Framework emphasizes the importance of risk management and encourages organizations to tailor their cybersecurity programs to their specific needs and risk profiles.

Another prominent security assessment framework is the Open Web Application Security Project (OWASP) Application Security Verification Standard (ASVS).

This framework is specifically focused on web application security and provides a set of security controls and requirements that organizations can use to assess the security of their web applications.

The ASVS covers a wide range of topics, including authentication, session management, access control, and data protection, making it a valuable resource for organizations that rely heavily on web applications.

For organizations looking to assess their overall information security management system, the International Organization for Standardization (ISO) 27001 framework is a widely recognized option.

ISO 27001 provides a systematic approach to managing information security risks and includes a comprehensive set of controls, policies, and procedures that organizations can implement to safeguard their information assets.

Achieving ISO 27001 certification demonstrates an organization's commitment to information security and can enhance its reputation with clients and partners.

While these frameworks are highly respected and widely used, there are also industry-specific frameworks that cater to the unique security needs of particular sectors.

For example, the Payment Card Industry Data Security Standard (PCI DSS) is designed to protect credit card data and is mandated for organizations that handle payment card transactions.

Similarly, the Health Insurance Portability and Accountability Act (HIPAA) Security Rule provides guidance on securing electronic protected health information (ePHI) for healthcare organizations.

In addition to these frameworks, there are specialized frameworks for critical infrastructure sectors, such as the North American Electric Reliability Corporation (NERC) Critical Infrastructure Protection (CIP) standards for the energy sector.

The adoption of a security assessment framework is not a one-time effort but rather an ongoing process that organizations should integrate into their cybersecurity practices.

It involves several key steps, starting with an initial assessment to establish a baseline of the organization's security posture.

This assessment typically involves identifying assets, assessing risks, and evaluating current security controls.

Once the baseline is established, organizations can prioritize security improvements based on the identified risks and vulnerabilities.

Implementing security controls and measures is a critical part of the process, as it involves the actual implementation of security policies, procedures, and technologies to mitigate risks.

Regular monitoring and testing are also essential components of a comprehensive security assessment framework.

This includes continuous monitoring of security controls, conducting vulnerability assessments, penetration testing, and security audits to ensure that security measures remain effective over time.

Incident response and recovery planning should also be integrated into the framework to prepare for and respond to security incidents effectively.

A well-defined incident response plan can minimize the impact of security breaches and aid in the recovery process.

Documentation and reporting play a crucial role in a comprehensive security assessment framework.

Organizations should maintain thorough records of their security assessments, vulnerabilities, and remediation efforts.

This documentation not only helps in tracking progress but also serves as evidence of compliance with relevant standards and regulations.

Additionally, reporting to senior management and stakeholders is essential to keep them informed about the organization's security posture and any potential risks.

Continuous improvement is a core principle of security assessment frameworks.

Organizations should regularly review and update their security measures, adapting to new threats and technologies.

This process includes conducting periodic risk assessments, reassessing the effectiveness of security controls, and adjusting security strategies accordingly.

Collaboration with internal and external stakeholders is vital for the success of a security assessment framework.

Effective communication and cooperation between IT teams, security teams, compliance officers, and third-party auditors can help align efforts and ensure that security goals are met.

Furthermore, engaging with industry peers and sharing best practices can enhance an organization's security posture.

In summary, comprehensive security assessment frameworks are instrumental in helping organizations evaluate and enhance their cybersecurity measures.

These frameworks provide structured methodologies, controls, and guidelines that enable organizations to assess their security posture, prioritize improvements, and continuously adapt to evolving threats.

By adopting and embracing security assessment frameworks, organizations can better protect their data, systems, and reputation in an increasingly complex and challenging cybersecurity landscape.

Tailoring audit methodologies to specific environments is a critical aspect of conducting effective and relevant security audits.

Every organization is unique, with its own set of objectives, technologies, and risk profiles, which means that a one-size-fits-all approach to security audits is often insufficient.

To ensure that security audits provide value and align with an organization's goals, auditors must customize their methodologies to fit the specific environment they are assessing.

One of the first steps in tailoring an audit methodology is understanding the organization's industry, business model, and regulatory requirements.

Different industries have distinct security challenges and compliance mandates, and auditors must be well-versed in the specific regulations that apply to the organization being audited.

For example, financial institutions may need to comply with regulations such as the Gramm-Leach-Bliley Act (GLBA), while healthcare organizations must adhere to the Health Insurance Portability and Accountability Act (HIPAA).

Understanding these industry-specific regulations is essential for auditors to evaluate an organization's compliance and security posture accurately.

In addition to industry considerations, auditors must also assess the organization's technology stack, infrastructure, and data flows.

This involves gaining insights into the organization's network architecture, the types of systems and applications in use, and the critical assets that need protection.

For example, a company heavily reliant on e-commerce may prioritize the security of its web applications, while a manufacturing firm may focus on securing its production systems.

The scope and depth of an audit may vary significantly based on the complexity of the organization's environment and the assets involved.

Once auditors have a clear understanding of the organization's context, they can tailor the audit methodology to address specific risks and vulnerabilities.

This customization may involve selecting appropriate assessment tools, techniques, and testing methodologies that align with the organization's technology stack and business processes.

For instance, if an organization relies heavily on cloud services, auditors should incorporate cloud security assessments into their methodology.

Moreover, auditors must consider the maturity level of the organization's security program.

A mature security program may require a more in-depth assessment with advanced penetration testing and red teaming exercises, while a less mature program may focus on fundamental security controls and awareness training.

Furthermore, auditors should engage with key stakeholders within the organization, including IT teams, security personnel, and executive management, to gather insights into their security concerns and priorities.

This collaborative approach ensures that the audit methodology reflects the organization's unique needs and that audit findings are relevant and actionable.

Risk assessment plays a central role in tailoring audit methodologies.

Auditors must identify and prioritize the most critical risks to the organization's security and focus their efforts accordingly.

This may involve conducting a risk assessment using methodologies like the National Institute of Standards and Technology (NIST) Risk Management Framework or the ISO 31000 standard.

By understanding the organization's risk landscape, auditors can develop a targeted audit plan that hones in on the areas of greatest concern.

Moreover, auditors should adapt their reporting and communication to meet the needs of the organization.

Some organizations may require highly technical reports with detailed vulnerability assessments and remediation recommendations, while others may prefer high-level executive summaries that emphasize business impact and risk mitigation.

The ability to communicate audit findings clearly and effectively is paramount in ensuring that stakeholders understand the security risks and the recommended actions to address them.

When tailoring audit methodologies, auditors should also consider the pace of technological change within the organization.

Technology evolves rapidly, and what may have been a best practice a year ago could be outdated today.

Auditors must stay up-to-date with emerging threats, attack vectors, and security controls to ensure that their assessments remain relevant.

This may involve attending industry conferences, participating in cybersecurity communities, and continuously expanding their knowledge.

Furthermore, auditors should be aware of cultural and organizational factors that can influence the audit process.

Organizations with a strong security culture may be more receptive to audit findings and proactive in addressing vulnerabilities.

On the other hand, organizations with a culture of resistance to change may require more effort in convincing stakeholders of the importance of security improvements.

In such cases, auditors should tailor their communication and engagement strategies to overcome resistance and drive positive change.

Lastly, it's essential to conduct post-audit reviews to assess the effectiveness of the audit methodology and identify areas for improvement.

This feedback loop ensures that audit methodologies continue to evolve and adapt to the changing needs of organizations.

In summary, tailoring audit methodologies to specific environments is crucial for conducting effective security audits that provide value and relevance to organizations.

By understanding the industry, technology stack, risk landscape, and organizational culture, auditors can customize their approaches, select appropriate assessment tools, and prioritize security risks effectively.

This customization ensures that audit findings are actionable and that organizations can address vulnerabilities and enhance their security posture with confidence.

Chapter 3: Exploiting Security Defenses

Identifying and overcoming advanced security measures is a complex and challenging task that requires a deep understanding of security systems and a creative approach to penetration testing.

In recent years, organizations have significantly enhanced their security defenses to protect against an evolving threat landscape, making it increasingly difficult for attackers to breach their systems.

As a result, ethical hackers and security professionals must continually update their skill sets and methodologies to identify and bypass these advanced security measures.

One of the fundamental steps in overcoming advanced security measures is reconnaissance, which involves gathering information about the target organization's security infrastructure, systems, and personnel.

This phase typically includes footprinting, scanning, and enumeration to identify potential vulnerabilities and weaknesses in the target's security posture.

In some cases, organizations may employ countermeasures such as intrusion detection systems (IDS) and intrusion prevention systems (IPS) to thwart reconnaissance efforts.

To overcome these countermeasures, ethical hackers may need to employ techniques like slow scanning or using decoy traffic to evade detection.

Once reconnaissance is complete, ethical hackers can proceed to the next stage, which involves identifying vulnerabilities in the target's systems and applications.

In the past, many organizations focused primarily on patch management to address vulnerabilities, but advanced security measures now include proactive measures such as threat hunting and continuous monitoring.

Ethical hackers must use a combination of automated vulnerability scanning tools and manual testing to uncover weaknesses that may not be readily apparent.

Furthermore, they may encounter web application firewalls (WAFs) and intrusion detection systems (IDS/IPS) designed to detect and block attacks.

To bypass these measures, ethical hackers can employ techniques like bypassing known WAF rules, using application-layer evasion techniques, and obfuscating their attacks.

Another challenge in overcoming advanced security measures is dealing with secure authentication and access control mechanisms.

Organizations increasingly adopt multi-factor authentication (MFA), strong password policies, and access controls based on the principle of least privilege (PoLP).

Ethical hackers may need to employ tactics such as password cracking, social engineering, or exploiting weak password reset procedures to gain unauthorized access.

Furthermore, they must stay informed about emerging authentication technologies and attack vectors to stay ahead of evolving security measures.

In addition to technical security measures, organizations often invest in security awareness training for their employees.

This includes phishing simulations and social engineering awareness programs designed to educate staff about potential security risks.

Ethical hackers may need to adapt their social engineering tactics to overcome the heightened awareness of employees, using more sophisticated and convincing techniques.

Moreover, organizations increasingly use endpoint security solutions, such as endpoint detection and response (EDR) systems, to monitor and protect their devices.

These solutions provide real-time visibility into endpoint activities, making it challenging for ethical hackers to operate undetected.

To overcome this obstacle, ethical hackers can leverage their knowledge of EDR systems to evade detection or manipulate endpoint logs to cover their tracks.

Advanced security measures also extend to network security, with organizations implementing robust intrusion detection and prevention systems (IDS/IPS) and next-generation firewalls (NGFW).

These security devices analyze network traffic for malicious activity and can automatically block suspicious traffic.

Ethical hackers must devise creative methods to evade detection by these systems, which may involve fragmentation attacks, tunneling, or encryption.

Furthermore, organizations may employ security information and event management (SIEM) solutions to centralize and analyze security logs.

These systems can detect anomalies and correlate events to identify potential security incidents.

Ethical hackers may need to manipulate or delete logs to avoid detection or employ advanced evasion techniques to evade SIEM monitoring.

In recent years, the adoption of cloud computing has introduced new challenges for ethical hackers.

Organizations move their infrastructure and data to cloud service providers (CSPs) like Amazon Web Services (AWS), Microsoft Azure, and Google Cloud Platform (GCP).

These CSPs offer robust security controls, but ethical hackers must understand cloud-specific security challenges, such as misconfigured permissions, shared responsibility models, and cloud-native attack vectors.

To overcome advanced cloud security measures, ethical hackers need to leverage tools and techniques designed for cloud environments and develop expertise in cloud security best practices.

Advanced security measures also extend to the detection and prevention of advanced persistent threats (APTs).

These threats are highly sophisticated and may remain undetected for extended periods.

Ethical hackers must employ tactics like threat hunting, behavioral analysis, and sandboxing to identify APTs and devise strategies to evade them.

Additionally, organizations increasingly employ threat intelligence feeds and information sharing platforms to stay informed about emerging threats.

Ethical hackers can use these resources to gain insights into the latest attack vectors and tactics used by threat actors.

Overcoming advanced security measures also involves understanding the legal and ethical considerations of penetration testing.

Ethical hackers must ensure they have proper authorization to conduct testing and respect privacy and data protection regulations.

They must also adhere to ethical guidelines and report vulnerabilities responsibly to organizations to facilitate remediation.

In summary, overcoming advanced security measures is a multifaceted challenge that requires a deep understanding of security technologies, continuous learning, and creative problem-solving.

Ethical hackers and security professionals must adapt their tactics and methodologies to bypass evolving security measures, whether they involve intrusion detection, authentication, endpoint security, or cloud-specific challenges.

Additionally, ethical conduct, respect for legal and ethical guidelines, and responsible vulnerability disclosure are essential aspects of overcoming advanced security measures in an ethical and productive manner.

Exploiting defense evasion techniques is a critical aspect of ethical hacking and penetration testing. In the ever-evolving landscape of cybersecurity, organizations deploy various defense mechanisms to protect their systems and data from unauthorized access and attacks.

These defense mechanisms include firewalls, intrusion detection systems (IDS), intrusion prevention systems (IPS), antivirus software, and endpoint security solutions.

To effectively test the security posture of an organization, ethical hackers must understand how these defenses work and, more importantly, how to bypass or evade them.

One common defense evasion technique employed by organizations is the use of firewalls. Firewalls are network security devices that monitor and control incoming and outgoing network traffic based on predefined security rules.

They can be either hardware or software-based and serve as a barrier between a trusted internal network and untrusted external networks, such as the internet.

Ethical hackers must be adept at identifying and exploiting weaknesses in firewall configurations. This might involve discovering open ports, exploiting protocol vulnerabilities, or using application-layer attacks to bypass firewall rules.

Another critical defense mechanism is intrusion detection systems (IDS) and intrusion prevention systems (IPS). IDS and IPS are designed to monitor network traffic for suspicious or malicious activity and can automatically block or alert on detected threats.

To evade these systems, ethical hackers must use techniques like traffic obfuscation, fragmentation, or encryption to hide their malicious traffic from detection.

Furthermore, they can craft packets or payloads that trigger false positives or negatives, leading to misclassification of the attack traffic.

Antivirus software is another layer of defense against malware and malicious code. Antivirus programs use signature-based detection and heuristic analysis to identify and quarantine malicious files.

Ethical hackers can evade antivirus detection by employing techniques like code obfuscation, polymorphic code, or custom encryption to make their malware undetectable.

Additionally, they can use fileless malware or in-memory attacks, which do not leave traces on disk, to avoid detection by traditional antivirus solutions.

Endpoint security solutions, such as endpoint detection and response (EDR) systems, are increasingly used by organizations to protect their devices from threats.

EDR solutions monitor endpoint activities and can detect and respond to suspicious behavior. Ethical hackers need to understand these solutions' capabilities and limitations to bypass or evade them.

This might involve disabling or bypassing EDR agents, manipulating logs, or using fileless malware that does not leave a trace on the endpoint.

Another crucial aspect of defense evasion is evading web application firewalls (WAFs). WAFs protect web applications from various attacks, including SQL injection, cross-site scripting (XSS), and cross-site request forgery (CSRF).

To bypass WAFs, ethical hackers can use techniques like input validation bypass, encoding and obfuscation, or leveraging vulnerabilities in the WAF itself.

Moreover, organizations employ security information and event management (SIEM) solutions to centralize and analyze security logs from various sources.

SIEM solutions can detect and correlate suspicious activities, making it challenging for attackers to operate undetected.

Ethical hackers must be familiar with SIEM solutions' capabilities and use techniques like log manipulation, log suppression, or evasion to avoid triggering alerts.

Additionally, organizations often employ deception technologies, such as honeypots and honeynets, to lure attackers and gather intelligence.

Ethical hackers can exploit deception technologies by identifying and avoiding these traps or by using them to their advantage to divert attention and resources from real attacks. Furthermore, defense evasion techniques extend to cloud security. With the increasing adoption of cloud computing, organizations must protect their cloud-based assets from threats.

Cloud security solutions, such as cloud access security brokers (CASBs) and cloud security posture management (CSPM) tools, help organizations monitor and secure their cloud environments.

Ethical hackers must understand these solutions' functionalities and bypass or evade them by exploiting misconfigurations, vulnerabilities, or cloud-native attack vectors.

Evasion techniques also encompass endpoint security evasion. Organizations often use host-based security solutions like application whitelisting and endpoint protection platforms (EPPs) to secure their devices.

Ethical hackers can evade these defenses by executing code in memory, leveraging trusted applications, or using living-off-the-land techniques to run malicious code without triggering alerts.

In summary, exploiting defense evasion techniques is a fundamental skill for ethical hackers and penetration testers.

To effectively assess an organization's security posture, ethical hackers must understand various defense mechanisms, including firewalls, IDS/IPS, antivirus software, endpoint security, WAFs, SIEM solutions, and cloud security.

By mastering the techniques to bypass or evade these defenses, ethical hackers can simulate real-world attack scenarios and help organizations identify and remediate vulnerabilities before malicious actors can exploit them.

Chapter 4: Mastering Penetration Testing Techniques

In the realm of ethical hacking and cybersecurity, advanced penetration testing tools and tactics play a pivotal role in assessing the security of systems, networks, and applications. These tools and techniques are instrumental in identifying vulnerabilities and weaknesses that malicious actors could exploit. Penetration testing, often referred to as pen testing or ethical hacking, is the practice of simulating cyberattacks on an organization's infrastructure to uncover security flaws.

Ethical hackers, who perform penetration testing, utilize an arsenal of cutting-edge tools and tactics to mimic the methods of malicious attackers while maintaining ethical boundaries.

One of the primary tools employed in advanced penetration testing is the use of vulnerability scanners. These scanners automatically identify and assess potential vulnerabilities in a target system or network. Ethical hackers rely on these tools to efficiently identify low-hanging fruits, such as outdated software, misconfigured settings, or known security issues.

To take penetration testing to the next level, ethical hackers often use more advanced vulnerability scanners that can perform in-depth analysis and provide detailed reports on the identified vulnerabilities. These tools help prioritize vulnerabilities based on their severity, allowing organizations to focus on the most critical issues first.

In addition to vulnerability scanners, ethical hackers leverage network analysis tools to gain insights into the target's network infrastructure. These tools help map out network topologies, identify active hosts, and discover potential entry points for attackers.

Advanced penetration testers go beyond simple network mapping and employ tactics like network sniffing to capture and analyze network traffic. By analyzing network packets, they can uncover sensitive information, detect security weaknesses, and identify potential attack vectors.

Exploitation frameworks are another critical component of advanced penetration testing. These frameworks, such as Metasploit, provide a wide range of pre-built exploits and payloads that can be used to compromise vulnerable systems. Ethical hackers can customize these exploits to suit the target environment, making them more effective in identifying and exploiting vulnerabilities.

While penetration testing tools are essential, it's equally important for ethical hackers to possess strong scripting and programming skills. Writing custom scripts and exploits allows them to tailor their attack vectors to specific targets and unique scenarios.

Web application penetration testing requires specialized tools and tactics. Web application scanners, like Burp Suite or OWASP ZAP, help ethical hackers assess the security of web applications by identifying vulnerabilities such as SQL injection, cross-site scripting (XSS), and insecure authentication mechanisms.

Advanced penetration testers conduct manual testing in tandem with automated tools to uncover complex vulnerabilities that may evade automated detection. They meticulously examine web applications, searching for weaknesses that automated scanners may overlook.

Social engineering plays a significant role in advanced penetration testing. Ethical hackers use social engineering tactics to manipulate individuals within the target organization into divulging sensitive information or performing actions that could compromise security.

Phishing campaigns, pretexting, and baiting are examples of social engineering techniques that ethical hackers employ to assess an organization's susceptibility to human manipulation. These tactics help identify weaknesses in employee awareness and training programs.

Advanced penetration testing also involves testing the security of wireless networks. Ethical hackers use tools like Aircrack-ng to assess the vulnerabilities of Wi-Fi networks, including weak encryption, default passwords, and improper configuration. By gaining unauthorized access to wireless networks, they can demonstrate the potential risks to an organization's data and resources.

To further their testing, ethical hackers engage in post-exploitation activities. Once they have compromised a system, they explore its internal environment to escalate privileges, move laterally through the network, and maintain persistent access. This phase simulates what malicious actors might do after gaining initial access.

Finally, reporting is a crucial aspect of advanced penetration testing. Ethical hackers meticulously document their findings, including detailed descriptions of vulnerabilities, exploitation steps, and potential impact. They provide actionable recommendations to help organizations remediate the identified issues and enhance their overall security posture.

In summary, advanced penetration testing tools and tactics are indispensable for ethical hackers in their mission to uncover vulnerabilities and enhance cybersecurity. By combining automated scanning tools, network analysis, exploitation frameworks, web application testing, social engineering, and post-exploitation activities, ethical hackers provide organizations with valuable insights into their security weaknesses and empower them to fortify their defenses against real-world threats.

In the realm of ethical hacking and penetration testing, post-exploitation and persistence strategies are critical components of simulating real-world cyberattacks and assessing the security of an organization's systems and networks.

Post-exploitation refers to the phase that occurs after an ethical hacker has successfully gained access to a target system or network.

During this phase, the ethical hacker focuses on maintaining a persistent presence, escalating privileges, and conducting further reconnaissance to gather valuable information.

The goal is to demonstrate the potential impact of a successful breach and the extent to which an attacker could compromise the target organization's assets.

One fundamental post-exploitation tactic is privilege escalation. Ethical hackers seek to escalate their privileges from standard user accounts to those with administrative or root-level access.

They do this by identifying and exploiting vulnerabilities or misconfigurations that allow them to gain higher-level privileges on the compromised system.

Privilege escalation techniques can include exploiting known vulnerabilities, abusing misconfigured permissions, or utilizing privilege escalation vulnerabilities specific to the target operating system.

Ethical hackers also aim to establish persistence on the compromised system, ensuring that they can maintain access even if the initial point of entry is discovered and remediated.

To achieve persistence, they may create backdoors, install rootkits, or set up scheduled tasks that provide them with a covert means of re-entry.

Additionally, ethical hackers often explore lateral movement within the network during the post-exploitation phase.

This involves navigating through the organization's systems and servers to gather valuable data and potentially compromise additional assets.

Lateral movement techniques can include exploiting vulnerabilities in network services, using stolen credentials, or abusing trust relationships between systems.

One critical aspect of post-exploitation is data exfiltration. Ethical hackers simulate the extraction of sensitive information, demonstrating how an attacker might steal valuable data from the compromised environment.

They utilize various methods for data exfiltration, such as transferring files over network protocols, encoding data within legitimate traffic, or exfiltrating data via covert channels.

Ethical hackers must also maintain stealth and avoid detection during post-exploitation activities.

They employ tactics like living off the land, using native system utilities, and evading security controls to remain undetected while navigating the compromised environment.

During this phase, ethical hackers often simulate the actions of advanced persistent threats (APTs), which are sophisticated adversaries known for their persistence and ability to remain hidden within a victim's network for extended periods.

The post-exploitation phase extends beyond the compromise of individual systems. Ethical hackers may target central servers, databases, and critical infrastructure components to assess the potential impact of a widespread breach.

Simulating post-exploitation scenarios helps organizations understand the importance of comprehensive security measures and the potential consequences of not addressing vulnerabilities and misconfigurations.

Furthermore, ethical hackers document their post-exploitation activities thoroughly. They create detailed reports that include the techniques used, the data accessed, the extent of lateral movement, and the potential business impact.

These reports are invaluable to organizations, as they provide a clear picture of the security risks posed by vulnerabilities and the steps required for remediation.

Ethical hackers also offer recommendations for improving security controls, enhancing monitoring, and fortifying defenses to prevent future breaches.

In summary, post-exploitation and persistence strategies are vital components of ethical hacking and penetration testing.

They enable ethical hackers to demonstrate the full extent of a successful breach, from privilege escalation to lateral movement, data exfiltration, and maintaining persistent access.

By simulating these scenarios, organizations gain valuable insights into their security weaknesses and can take proactive measures to enhance their security posture and protect against real-world threats.

Chapter 5: Web Application Security Auditing

In the ever-evolving landscape of cybersecurity, web application vulnerabilities continue to be a prominent concern for organizations and individuals alike.

Web applications, ranging from e-commerce platforms and social media networks to online banking portals and content management systems, have become integral parts of our daily lives.

However, the very nature of these applications, which are accessible via the internet, makes them susceptible to a wide range of security threats and vulnerabilities.

This chapter delves into an in-depth analysis of common web application vulnerabilities, shedding light on the risks they pose and the techniques used to exploit them.

One of the most prevalent web application vulnerabilities is known as Cross-Site Scripting (XSS).

XSS occurs when an attacker injects malicious scripts into a web application, which are then executed by unsuspecting users.

These scripts can steal sensitive user data, hijack user sessions, deface websites, or even distribute malware to visitors.

There are three main types of XSS: stored, reflected, and DOM-based, each with its own attack vector and impact.

Another critical web application vulnerability is SQL Injection (SQLi).

SQLi occurs when an attacker manipulates input fields or parameters of a web application to inject malicious SQL queries into the database.

Successful SQLi attacks can provide unauthorized access to the database, allowing attackers to retrieve, modify, or delete sensitive data.

SQLi vulnerabilities often arise from improper input validation and inadequate security controls.

Cross-Site Request Forgery (CSRF) is another web application vulnerability where an attacker tricks a user into performing unwanted actions without their knowledge.

This can result in unauthorized actions being taken on behalf of the victim, such as changing passwords, making financial transactions, or altering account settings.

Insecure Deserialization is a web application vulnerability that arises when an application improperly handles serialized data.

Attackers can manipulate serialized objects to execute arbitrary code, potentially leading to remote code execution and compromise of the application or server.

Security Misconfigurations are a broad category of web application vulnerabilities that occur due to improperly configured settings, permissions, or access controls.

These vulnerabilities can lead to unauthorized access, data exposure, or even full system compromise.

Examples of security misconfigurations include exposed administrative interfaces, unnecessary open ports, and overly permissive file permissions.

Broken Authentication is a web application vulnerability where an attacker exploits flaws in the authentication and session management processes.

This can result in unauthorized access to user accounts, impersonation, or session hijacking.

Vulnerable libraries and components are often overlooked sources of web application vulnerabilities.

When web applications use outdated or poorly maintained libraries, attackers can exploit known vulnerabilities in these components to compromise the application or server.

Insecure Direct Object References (IDOR) occur when an attacker can manipulate references to objects, such as files or database records, to access unauthorized data.

This vulnerability can lead to data leaks and unauthorized access to sensitive information.

Security headers play a crucial role in web application security.

The absence or misconfiguration of security headers can leave web applications vulnerable to various attacks, such as clickjacking, cross-site scripting, and content injection.

XML External Entity (XXE) vulnerabilities arise when an attacker can control the processing of XML data.

By exploiting XXE, an attacker can read files, perform internal port scanning, or launch denial-of-service attacks against the server.

Broken Access Control is a web application vulnerability that occurs when improper or insufficient access controls allow users to perform actions they shouldn't.

This can lead to unauthorized access to sensitive data or functionality.

Unvalidated Redirects and Forwards are vulnerabilities that allow attackers to redirect users to malicious websites or execute unwanted actions.

These vulnerabilities often exploit flaws in URL redirection mechanisms.

File Upload vulnerabilities arise when an application allows users to upload files without proper validation and controls.

Attackers can upload malicious files, leading to various security risks, including remote code execution.

To mitigate web application vulnerabilities, organizations should adopt a proactive approach to security.

This includes implementing secure coding practices, performing regular security assessments, and staying informed about emerging threats and vulnerabilities.

Web application firewalls (WAFs) are commonly used to protect against known attacks and provide an additional layer of defense.

Regularly patching and updating web application components, libraries, and frameworks is essential to address known vulnerabilities.

Security testing, including dynamic and static analysis, can help identify and remediate vulnerabilities in web applications.

Penetration testing and code review are valuable tools in assessing and improving the security of web applications.

Ultimately, web application vulnerabilities pose significant risks to organizations and individuals, making it imperative to understand these vulnerabilities, employ best practices in web application development, and maintain vigilant security measures to protect against exploitation and data breaches.

In the realm of security auditing and vulnerability assessment, two primary approaches exist: manual and automated.

Each approach has its advantages and limitations, and the choice between them often depends on the specific goals and resources of an organization.

Manual auditing involves the use of human expertise to assess and analyze an organization's systems, networks, and applications.

This approach relies on skilled professionals, often referred to as ethical hackers or penetration testers, who manually explore and test the security of a target environment.

Manual auditing allows for a comprehensive evaluation of an organization's security posture, as it involves in-depth analysis, creativity, and adaptability.

Ethical hackers conducting manual audits can identify vulnerabilities that automated tools might overlook, such as complex business logic flaws or novel attack vectors.

Additionally, manual auditing can simulate the actions of real-world attackers, providing valuable insights into how an organization's defenses would fare against sophisticated adversaries.

One of the key advantages of manual auditing is the ability to customize the assessment based on the specific needs and goals of the organization.

Ethical hackers can tailor their testing methodologies to target critical assets, assess unique business processes, and address specific concerns.

This level of customization allows organizations to focus on their most pressing security challenges and gain a deeper understanding of their vulnerabilities.

Furthermore, manual auditing is particularly effective in assessing the human element of security, such as social engineering vulnerabilities or insider threats.

Ethical hackers can simulate phishing attacks, conduct physical security assessments, and evaluate the effectiveness of security awareness training programs.

However, manual auditing also has its limitations.

It can be time-consuming and resource-intensive, as it requires skilled professionals to manually conduct assessments, analyze findings, and generate reports.

The expertise of ethical hackers is a critical factor in the success of manual audits, and organizations may face challenges in finding and retaining qualified professionals.

Additionally, manual audits may not scale well for large and complex environments, where automated tools can provide more efficiency and coverage.

In contrast, automated auditing relies on security tools and software to scan, analyze, and assess an organization's systems and networks.

These tools can quickly identify known vulnerabilities, misconfigurations, and security weaknesses across a wide range of assets.

Automated auditing is efficient and can cover a large number of systems in a relatively short amount of time.

It is well-suited for continuous monitoring, allowing organizations to regularly scan their infrastructure for new vulnerabilities and potential threats.

Automated tools can provide consistent and repeatable results, reducing the potential for human error and ensuring thorough coverage of assets.

However, automated auditing has its limitations as well.

It is primarily effective at identifying known vulnerabilities and may struggle to detect novel or zero-day threats.

Automated tools rely on vulnerability databases and known attack patterns, so they may not uncover vulnerabilities that have not been previously documented.

Furthermore, automated auditing may generate false positives, flagging issues that do not pose a real security risk.

This can lead to alert fatigue and wasted resources as security teams investigate non-issues.

Another challenge with automated auditing is that it may not fully capture the context and nuances of an organization's environment.

While it can identify vulnerabilities, it may not understand the business logic or unique processes that influence the risk associated with those vulnerabilities.

Ultimately, the choice between manual and automated auditing approaches depends on the specific goals and circumstances of an organization.

Many organizations opt for a hybrid approach, combining the strengths of both manual and automated methods.

They use automated tools to perform regular scans and identify known vulnerabilities, while also engaging ethical hackers for periodic manual assessments to uncover complex or novel threats.

This hybrid approach allows organizations to benefit from the efficiency of automation while leveraging human expertise for in-depth analysis and tailored assessments.

In summary, manual and automated auditing approaches each have their merits and drawbacks, and organizations should carefully consider their goals, resources, and risk tolerance when choosing an auditing strategy.

Both approaches play a crucial role in maintaining a strong security posture and protecting against evolving threats in today's dynamic cybersecurity landscape.

Chapter 6: Advanced Wireless Network Assessment

In today's interconnected world, Wi-Fi networks have become ubiquitous, providing wireless access to the internet and local resources.

However, with the convenience of Wi-Fi comes the challenge of securing these networks against a wide range of threats and potential vulnerabilities.

This chapter explores advanced Wi-Fi hacking techniques and the security measures necessary to defend against them.

One of the most common Wi-Fi hacking techniques is known as "password cracking."

Attackers use specialized software to attempt to guess the Wi-Fi network's pre-shared key or password.

They may employ techniques like brute-force attacks, dictionary attacks, or rainbow tables to crack weak or easily guessable passwords.

To defend against password cracking attacks, it's essential to use strong, complex passwords for Wi-Fi networks.

This includes a combination of upper and lower-case letters, numbers, and special characters.

Additionally, it's crucial to avoid using easily guessable phrases or dictionary words as passwords.

Another common Wi-Fi hacking technique is "WPS PIN brute-forcing."

Wi-Fi Protected Setup (WPS) is a feature designed to simplify the process of connecting devices to a Wi-Fi network.

However, WPS PINs can be exploited by attackers who use brute-force methods to guess the eight-digit PIN required for access.

To secure against WPS PIN brute-forcing attacks, it's advisable to disable WPS entirely if it's not needed for your network.

Alternatively, some routers allow you to lock out an attacker after a certain number of failed PIN attempts.

An advanced Wi-Fi hacking technique involves "man-in-the-middle" (MitM) attacks.

In these attacks, an attacker intercepts and relays communication between a victim's device and the Wi-Fi network, allowing them to eavesdrop on sensitive data.

Common MitM attacks against Wi-Fi networks include ARP spoofing and DNS spoofing.

To protect against MitM attacks, use encryption protocols like WPA3, which provides robust encryption and protection against eavesdropping.

Implementing secure practices for Wi-Fi networks is essential, such as using strong encryption, regularly changing Wi-Fi passwords, and configuring routers to use secure DNS servers.

Another Wi-Fi hacking technique is "rogue access points."

In this scenario, an attacker sets up a malicious Wi-Fi network with a legitimate-sounding name to trick users into connecting.

Once connected, the attacker can intercept and manipulate the traffic of connected devices.

To defend against rogue access points, implement wireless intrusion detection systems (WIDS) that can detect unauthorized access points and take action to block them.

"Evil Twin" attacks are a variation of rogue access point attacks.

In an Evil Twin attack, an attacker sets up a malicious Wi-Fi network with the same name and credentials as a legitimate network.

Unsuspecting users may inadvertently connect to the Evil Twin network, allowing the attacker to capture their data.

To protect against Evil Twin attacks, educate users about the importance of verifying the legitimacy of Wi-Fi networks before connecting and use strong encryption protocols.

Wi-Fi phishing attacks involve tricking users into providing their Wi-Fi credentials through phishing emails or fake login portals. Attackers send emails that appear to be from legitimate sources, prompting users to enter their Wi-Fi usernames and passwords.

To guard against Wi-Fi phishing attacks, educate users about phishing awareness and encourage them to verify the authenticity of email requests for Wi-Fi credentials.

Wi-Fi deauthentication and disassociation attacks are techniques used to disrupt Wi-Fi connections.

Attackers send deauthentication or disassociation packets to disconnect users from a Wi-Fi network.

To mitigate such attacks, network administrators can implement intrusion detection systems (IDS) that monitor for unusual behavior and respond to deauthentication attacks.

Advanced Wi-Fi hacking techniques can also target the vulnerabilities of specific Wi-Fi protocols.

For example, the "KRACK" (Key Reinstallation Attack) targets the WPA2 protocol's vulnerabilities.

KRACK attacks manipulate the process of establishing encryption keys, allowing attackers to intercept and decrypt traffic on a WPA2-protected network.

To protect against KRACK attacks, it's crucial to keep Wi-Fi devices and routers updated with security patches and, if possible, upgrade to the more secure WPA3 protocol.

While this chapter has explored advanced Wi-Fi hacking techniques, it's essential to emphasize that the best defense against such attacks is a strong security posture.

Implementing strong encryption, using complex passwords, and regularly updating Wi-Fi devices and routers are fundamental practices for securing Wi-Fi networks.

Additionally, educating users about Wi-Fi security risks and best practices plays a critical role in overall network security.

In the ever-evolving landscape of cybersecurity, staying informed about the latest threats and vulnerabilities is essential to adapting and defending against advanced Wi-Fi hacking techniques.

By taking proactive measures and staying vigilant, individuals and organizations can safeguard their Wi-Fi networks and the data transmitted over them from malicious actors and potential security breaches.

Wireless networks have become an integral part of our daily lives, offering the convenience of untethered connectivity.

However, this convenience also brings security challenges, making wireless network intrusion detection and prevention crucial for safeguarding sensitive data.

Intrusion detection and prevention systems (IDPS) are essential components of network security.

In the realm of wireless networks, these systems play a vital role in identifying and thwarting potential threats.

One of the primary functions of wireless network intrusion detection systems is to monitor network traffic.

By analyzing packets of data transmitted over the wireless network, the IDPS can identify patterns and anomalies that may indicate a security breach.

These anomalies might include unexpected traffic spikes, suspicious connection attempts, or unauthorized access to network resources.

To effectively detect intrusions, IDPSs rely on various detection techniques.

One common approach is signature-based detection, where the system looks for predefined patterns or signatures associated with known attacks.

For example, the IDPS may search for patterns in network traffic that match the characteristics of a known malware or intrusion attempt.

Behavior-based detection is another technique employed by wireless network intrusion detection systems.

In this approach, the system learns the normal behavior of the network and its users over time.

When it detects deviations from this baseline behavior, it raises an alert, as these deviations may indicate an intrusion or unauthorized activity.

Wireless network intrusion detection systems can also utilize anomaly-based detection.

This method involves looking for unusual or unexpected patterns in network traffic.

For instance, a sudden surge in traffic from a single user or a device attempting to communicate with a large number of different devices could be indicative of an attack.

While intrusion detection systems are designed to identify potential threats, intrusion prevention systems (IPS) take it a step further by actively blocking or mitigating those threats.

In wireless networks, IPSs work to stop malicious activity in its tracks.

When the system detects an intrusion attempt or suspicious behavior, it can take immediate action to block the source of the threat.

For example, an IPS might block a specific IP address or MAC address that is attempting to exploit a vulnerability or launch an attack.

Wireless network intrusion prevention systems are often configured to take predefined actions, such as dropping malicious packets, disconnecting compromised devices, or altering firewall rules to protect the network.

To effectively deploy wireless network intrusion detection and prevention systems, organizations must consider various factors.

One critical factor is the placement of sensors or monitoring points within the network.

These sensors capture network traffic and send it to the IDPS/IPS for analysis.

Careful placement of sensors is essential to ensure comprehensive coverage and the early detection of threats.

Organizations must also establish clear security policies and rules for their wireless networks.

These policies should define acceptable use, access control, and authentication mechanisms.

Additionally, regular monitoring and maintenance of the intrusion detection and prevention systems are vital to keeping them up to date and effective.

An essential element of wireless network security is encryption.

Encrypting wireless traffic ensures that even if an attacker intercepts the data, they cannot decipher it without the encryption keys.

The use of protocols like WPA3 for Wi-Fi encryption adds an extra layer of security.

However, encryption alone is not sufficient; intrusion detection and prevention systems are necessary to monitor encrypted traffic for signs of intrusion.

Wireless network intrusion detection and prevention systems can also aid in identifying rogue access points.

Rogue access points are unauthorized wireless devices or networks that pose a security risk.

These devices can be set up by malicious actors to trick users into connecting, potentially exposing sensitive data.

IDPSs can detect and report the presence of rogue access points, allowing organizations to take action and mitigate the threat.

Additionally, wireless network intrusion detection systems are crucial for identifying denial-of-service (DoS) and distributed denial-of-service (DDoS) attacks.

These attacks flood a wireless network with traffic, overwhelming its capacity and rendering it unavailable to legitimate users.

By detecting and mitigating these attacks, IDPSs and IPSs help maintain network availability and prevent service disruptions.

It's important to note that the landscape of wireless network threats is constantly evolving.

Attackers are continually developing new techniques and exploits to compromise wireless networks.

Therefore, wireless network intrusion detection and prevention systems must receive regular updates to stay effective against emerging threats.

Furthermore, organizations should invest in skilled personnel who can interpret the alerts generated by these systems and respond to potential incidents promptly.

In summary, wireless network intrusion detection and prevention systems are indispensable tools for securing wireless networks.

They play a vital role in identifying and mitigating threats, protecting sensitive data, and ensuring the availability and integrity of wireless networks.

By implementing robust intrusion detection and prevention strategies, organizations can defend against a wide range of wireless network threats and stay one step ahead of attackers.

Chapter 7: Cloud Security Auditing

Auditing cloud service models, including Infrastructure as a Service (IaaS), Platform as a Service (PaaS), and Software as a Service (SaaS), is essential for organizations embracing cloud technology.

As businesses increasingly rely on cloud computing, understanding the unique challenges and risks associated with each service model is crucial.

Infrastructure as a Service, or IaaS, is the foundational layer of cloud services, providing virtualized computing resources over the internet.

Auditing IaaS involves assessing the security and compliance controls implemented by cloud service providers (CSPs) to protect the underlying infrastructure.

Security considerations in IaaS audits include evaluating the physical security of data centers, access controls, and data encryption practices.

PaaS, or Platform as a Service, builds upon IaaS by offering a development platform and tools that enable the creation and deployment of applications.

Auditing PaaS involves assessing the security of the development environment, the effectiveness of access controls, and the protection of application data.

Security audits in PaaS may focus on identity and access management (IAM) solutions, application security testing, and data encryption within applications.

Software as a Service, or SaaS, delivers fully functional software applications over the internet.

SaaS audits concentrate on assessing the security of these applications and the data they handle.

Auditors must evaluate user authentication and authorization mechanisms, data protection measures, and the vendor's adherence to security best practices.

When conducting cloud service audits, it's crucial to consider the shared responsibility model.

Under this model, the CSP and the customer share responsibilities for security, with the exact division varying depending on the service model.

For IaaS, the CSP is typically responsible for securing the physical infrastructure and the hypervisor, while the customer is responsible for securing their virtual machines and applications.

In PaaS, the CSP secures the platform, while the customer secures their applications and data.

SaaS providers typically handle most security aspects, but customers are responsible for securing their access to the service and ensuring proper data usage.

Auditors should thoroughly review service level agreements (SLAs) to understand the responsibilities of both parties.

One of the primary goals of auditing cloud service models is to ensure compliance with relevant regulations and standards.

Many industries have specific compliance requirements, such as HIPAA for healthcare or PCI DSS for payment card data.

Auditors must assess whether the chosen cloud service model aligns with these compliance requirements.

For example, a healthcare organization using a cloud-based Electronic Health Record (EHR) system must verify that the SaaS provider complies with HIPAA regulations.

Auditing cloud service models also entails assessing data governance practices.

This includes evaluating how data is stored, processed, and transmitted within the cloud environment.

Auditors must ensure that data is classified appropriately, access controls are enforced, and data encryption is implemented where necessary.

Data residency and sovereignty considerations are essential, especially when dealing with international cloud providers.

To effectively audit cloud service models, organizations should establish a cloud governance framework that outlines roles, responsibilities, and procedures.

This framework helps ensure that cloud services are provisioned and managed in a secure and compliant manner. Regularly scheduled audits and assessments should be part of this governance framework to monitor ongoing compliance and security.

In addition to compliance and security, auditing cloud service models should also focus on performance and cost optimization.

Evaluating the efficiency of resource allocation, monitoring usage, and optimizing cloud spend are essential components of cloud service audits.

Organizations must ensure that cloud resources are allocated appropriately to meet their performance requirements while minimizing unnecessary expenses.

When auditing IaaS, considerations include the provisioning of virtual machines, storage, and network resources.

In PaaS, the focus shifts to evaluating the efficiency of development and deployment processes.

For SaaS, audits should assess whether the subscription aligns with actual usage and whether users have the necessary access.

Auditing cloud service models requires a multi-faceted approach that addresses technical, compliance, security, and financial aspects.

It's crucial to collaborate with experienced auditors who understand cloud technologies and the unique challenges they present.

Furthermore, organizations should leverage automated tools and cloud-native solutions for monitoring and auditing to streamline the process and improve efficiency.

By conducting regular audits of cloud service models, organizations can harness the benefits of cloud computing while mitigating risks and ensuring compliance with industry regulations.

Ensuring compliance and security in cloud environments is a paramount concern for organizations of all sizes and industries.

As businesses increasingly migrate their IT infrastructure and services to the cloud, they must address the unique challenges that come with this transformation.

One of the primary challenges is understanding the shared responsibility model, which defines the responsibilities of both cloud service providers (CSPs) and their customers in terms of security and compliance.

In this model, CSPs are responsible for the security of the cloud infrastructure, including data centers, networking, and the physical security of hardware.

Customers, on the other hand, are responsible for securing their data and applications that run on the cloud platform.

It's essential for organizations to clearly delineate these responsibilities to avoid gaps in security and compliance coverage.

To ensure compliance in cloud environments, organizations must first identify the relevant regulations and standards that apply to their industry and geographical location.

For example, healthcare organizations must comply with the Health Insurance Portability and Accountability Act (HIPAA), while financial institutions must adhere to the Payment Card Industry Data Security Standard (PCI DSS).

Understanding these requirements is crucial for developing a comprehensive compliance strategy.

Once the regulatory landscape is clear, organizations can work with CSPs to assess their compliance with relevant standards.

CSPs often undergo third-party audits and assessments to demonstrate their adherence to security and compliance frameworks.

Reviewing these audit reports and certifications is a critical step in ensuring that a CSP's services meet the necessary compliance requirements.

In addition to CSP compliance, organizations must also evaluate their own compliance efforts.

This includes assessing whether the cloud environment aligns with their internal policies and procedures and complies with industry-specific regulations.

Cloud environments should be treated as an extension of the organization's infrastructure, and the same compliance controls should be applied.

One essential aspect of ensuring security in cloud environments is identity and access management (IAM).

IAM solutions help organizations control who has access to their cloud resources and data.

Effective IAM includes user provisioning, role-based access control, multi-factor authentication, and robust password policies.

Organizations should implement IAM best practices to prevent unauthorized access and data breaches.

Another crucial consideration is data encryption.

Data at rest, in transit, and during processing should be encrypted to protect it from unauthorized access.

Organizations should use encryption mechanisms provided by their CSP and implement encryption practices within their applications and databases.

Monitoring and auditing cloud environments are fundamental to maintaining compliance and security.

Continuous monitoring tools can provide real-time insights into the state of the cloud infrastructure, helping organizations detect and respond to security incidents promptly.

Regular audits and assessments should be conducted to evaluate the effectiveness of security controls and compliance efforts.

In addition to internal audits, organizations should consider engaging third-party auditors to provide an objective assessment of their cloud security and compliance posture.

Cloud providers offer a range of security services and tools that can enhance security and compliance efforts.

These include security information and event management (SIEM) solutions, threat detection services, and security analytics tools.

Leveraging these services can help organizations proactively identify and mitigate security threats.

Security incident response plans are essential for cloud environments.

Organizations should have well-defined incident response procedures in place to address security incidents effectively.

These plans should include roles and responsibilities, incident detection and reporting, containment, eradication, and recovery strategies.

Cloud environments also benefit from the implementation of a robust security awareness and training program for employees.

Security awareness training helps employees recognize and respond to security threats, reducing the likelihood of insider threats and social engineering attacks.

Additionally, organizations should regularly update and patch their cloud resources to address known vulnerabilities. Cloud providers often release security updates and patches, and organizations should promptly apply these to mitigate risks.

Ensuring compliance and security in cloud environments is an ongoing effort that requires vigilance and dedication.

Organizations must stay informed about emerging threats and evolving regulations to adapt their security and compliance strategies accordingly.

Collaboration with CSPs and third-party experts can provide valuable insights and guidance in this ever-changing landscape.

By taking a proactive approach to security and compliance in the cloud, organizations can reap the benefits of cloud computing while safeguarding their data and reputation.

Chapter 8: Insider Threat Detection and Response

Advanced insider threat detection techniques are crucial in today's cybersecurity landscape, where the risk of insider threats continues to grow.

Insider threats, which can come from employees, contractors, or business partners, pose a significant risk to organizations, and traditional security measures are often insufficient in detecting and mitigating these threats.

To address this challenge, organizations are adopting advanced techniques that go beyond basic security controls and leverage cutting-edge technology and methodologies.

One of the key components of advanced insider threat detection is the use of behavioral analytics.

Behavioral analytics involves the continuous monitoring of user activities and the analysis of behavioral patterns to identify deviations from the norm.

By establishing a baseline of normal user behavior, organizations can detect anomalies that may indicate malicious or unauthorized activities.

Behavioral analytics tools use machine learning and artificial intelligence to analyze vast amounts of data, making it possible to detect subtle and sophisticated insider threats.

User and entity behavior analytics (UEBA) is a subset of behavioral analytics that focuses on identifying abnormal behavior related to both users and entities, such as devices or applications.

UEBA solutions use algorithms to detect suspicious activities, such as a user accessing sensitive data at unusual times or from unfamiliar locations.

Another advanced insider threat detection technique is the use of data loss prevention (DLP) solutions.

DLP technology helps organizations monitor and control the movement of sensitive data within and outside their networks.

By classifying data and defining policies, DLP solutions can detect and prevent unauthorized data transfers or leaks that may be indicative of insider threats.

Endpoint detection and response (EDR) solutions play a critical role in advanced insider threat detection.

EDR solutions provide real-time monitoring and response capabilities at the endpoint level, enabling organizations to detect and contain insider threats quickly.

These solutions collect and analyze endpoint data, allowing security teams to identify suspicious activities, investigate incidents, and respond effectively.

Machine learning and artificial intelligence are integral to advanced insider threat detection.

Machine learning models can analyze vast datasets to identify patterns and anomalies, making it possible to detect subtle signs of insider threats that might go unnoticed by traditional security tools.

These models can also adapt and improve their accuracy over time as they learn from new data.

User and entity behavior analytics, as mentioned earlier, heavily rely on machine learning to identify unusual patterns of behavior that may indicate insider threats.

Natural language processing (NLP) is another technology used in advanced insider threat detection.

NLP enables organizations to analyze and understand unstructured data sources, such as email communications and chat logs.

By applying NLP techniques, organizations can identify suspicious language or content that may suggest insider threats, such as employees discussing unauthorized activities.

Continuous monitoring is a fundamental aspect of advanced insider threat detection.

Rather than conducting periodic security assessments, organizations implement real-time monitoring solutions that provide constant visibility into their networks, systems, and data.

This continuous monitoring allows security teams to detect insider threats as they happen and respond promptly to mitigate the risks.

Network traffic analysis is essential for advanced insider threat detection.

By analyzing network traffic, organizations can identify unusual or unauthorized activities that may indicate insider threats.

Advanced network monitoring solutions can detect data exfiltration attempts, unauthorized access to sensitive resources, or lateral movement within the network.

Collaborative security intelligence is a rising trend in advanced insider threat detection.

Organizations are sharing threat intelligence and collaborating with industry peers to enhance their ability to detect and respond to insider threats.

By pooling resources and knowledge, organizations can gain insights into new threats and vulnerabilities that may be used by malicious insiders.

Integration and automation play a vital role in advanced insider threat detection.

Organizations are integrating their security tools and platforms to create a unified security ecosystem that can detect, investigate, and respond to insider threats seamlessly.

Automation streamlines incident response processes, allowing organizations to react quickly to insider threats and minimize their impact.

Machine learning models can automate the analysis of large datasets, while orchestration tools can coordinate responses across various security tools.

Advanced insider threat detection requires a holistic approach that combines technology, processes, and people.

Organizations must establish clear policies and procedures for identifying and responding to insider threats, and they must provide training and awareness programs for employees to recognize and report suspicious activities.

Additionally, organizations should conduct regular security audits and assessments to evaluate the effectiveness of their insider threat detection efforts.

In summary, advanced insider threat detection techniques are essential for organizations to protect against the growing risk of insider threats.

These techniques leverage behavioral analytics, machine learning, data loss prevention, endpoint detection and response, and other advanced technologies to detect and respond to insider threats effectively.

By adopting a proactive and integrated approach to insider threat detection, organizations can safeguard their sensitive data and intellectual property from malicious insiders.

Incident response strategies for insider threats are a critical component of any organization's cybersecurity program.

Insider threats, which can come from employees, contractors, or business partners, have the potential to cause significant harm to an organization's data, systems, and reputation.

Effective incident response strategies are essential for detecting, mitigating, and recovering from insider threat incidents.

One of the fundamental principles of incident response is preparation.

Organizations should have a well-defined incident response plan in place, specifically tailored to address insider threats.

This plan should outline roles and responsibilities, communication procedures, and the steps to be taken when an insider threat is detected.

The incident response team should consist of individuals with expertise in cybersecurity, legal, human resources, and law enforcement, if necessary.

In the event of an insider threat incident, a coordinated response is essential to minimize the impact and protect the organization.

Detection is a critical phase of incident response, and this is especially true for insider threats.

Organizations should deploy advanced monitoring and detection tools to identify unusual or suspicious activities that may indicate an insider threat.

Behavioral analytics, user and entity behavior analytics (UEBA), and machine learning models can help identify deviations from normal behavior patterns, enabling the early detection of insider threats.

When an insider threat is detected, organizations should follow a well-defined escalation process.

This process should involve notifying the incident response team, relevant stakeholders, and, if necessary, law enforcement agencies.

Communication is key during this phase to ensure that all necessary parties are informed and can take appropriate action.

Once an insider threat incident is confirmed, containment measures should be implemented swiftly.

This may involve isolating the affected systems, revoking access privileges, and taking steps to prevent further damage or data loss.

The goal is to limit the insider's ability to continue their malicious activities.

Investigation is a crucial phase of incident response for insider threats.

Organizations should conduct a thorough investigation to determine the extent of the breach, the motives of the insider, and the potential impact on sensitive data or critical systems.

Forensic analysis may be required to gather evidence and build a case for legal action if necessary.

Legal considerations are paramount when dealing with insider threat incidents.

Organizations must work closely with their legal counsel to ensure that all actions taken during the incident response process comply with applicable laws and regulations.

This may involve notifying affected individuals or regulatory authorities, depending on the nature and scope of the incident.

Communication with affected parties is an essential aspect of incident response for insider threats.

Organizations should develop a communication plan that includes messaging to employees, customers, partners, and other stakeholders, as appropriate.

Transparency and honesty in communication can help rebuild trust and mitigate reputational damage.

Recovery efforts should begin once the insider threat incident has been contained and investigated.

This may involve restoring affected systems, implementing security improvements, and addressing any vulnerabilities or weaknesses that were exploited by the insider.

Organizations should also evaluate the effectiveness of their incident response plan and make necessary adjustments to enhance future readiness.

Learning from the incident is essential for continuous improvement.

Post-incident analysis should include a detailed review of the incident response process to identify areas for improvement.

This may involve evaluating the effectiveness of detection mechanisms, response times, and the overall coordination of the incident response team.

Sharing lessons learned can benefit the organization and the broader cybersecurity community.

Continuous monitoring and ongoing threat intelligence are essential for preventing future insider threats.

Organizations should invest in tools and technologies that can help identify insider threat indicators in real time.

User behavior analytics and anomaly detection can assist in proactively identifying potential insider threats before they escalate.

Employee training and awareness programs are critical components of insider threat prevention.

Organizations should educate their employees about the risks of insider threats, the importance of reporting suspicious activities, and the consequences of insider misconduct.

Whistleblower programs can provide employees with a safe and confidential means to report concerns.

Insider threat incidents can be complex and challenging to resolve.

Organizations should consider seeking external expertise, such as cybersecurity consulting firms or forensic investigators, to assist with incident response and investigation efforts.

In summary, incident response strategies for insider threats are vital for organizations to effectively address the risks posed by malicious insiders.

Preparation, detection, escalation, containment, investigation, legal considerations, communication, recovery, and continuous improvement are all integral elements of a robust insider threat incident response plan.

By following these principles and incorporating best practices, organizations can better protect their data, systems, and reputation from insider threats.

Chapter 9: Auditing for Compliance and Regulations

Navigating regulatory frameworks and compliance standards is a crucial aspect of modern business operations.

Organizations in various industries must adhere to a complex web of regulations, laws, and standards that govern their activities.

These regulations and standards are designed to ensure transparency, fairness, and ethical behavior in business practices.

Failure to comply with these requirements can result in legal consequences, financial penalties, and damage to an organization's reputation.

To successfully navigate regulatory frameworks, organizations must first understand the specific regulations that apply to their industry and geographical location.

Different countries and regions have their own sets of regulations, which can vary widely.

It is essential for organizations to conduct thorough research and engage legal experts who specialize in regulatory compliance to gain a comprehensive understanding of their obligations.

Regulatory compliance is often categorized into two main types: industry-specific regulations and cross-industry regulations.

Industry-specific regulations are tailored to a particular sector, such as healthcare, finance, or telecommunications.

These regulations address industry-specific challenges and risks and often require specialized compliance measures.

Cross-industry regulations, on the other hand, apply to all organizations regardless of their sector.

Examples include data protection regulations like the General Data Protection Regulation (GDPR) and anti-money laundering laws.

Organizations must identify which cross-industry regulations are relevant to their operations and take appropriate steps to comply.

One of the fundamental principles of navigating regulatory frameworks is proactive compliance.

Rather than waiting for regulatory authorities to enforce compliance, organizations should proactively implement measures to meet regulatory requirements.

This approach not only reduces the risk of non-compliance but also demonstrates a commitment to ethical business practices.

To achieve proactive compliance, organizations should establish a compliance management framework.

This framework includes policies, procedures, and controls designed to ensure that all relevant regulations are followed.

It also involves assigning responsibilities to individuals within the organization to oversee compliance efforts.

Regular audits and assessments are essential components of a compliance management framework.

These evaluations help organizations identify areas where compliance may be lacking and take corrective action promptly.

Regulatory bodies often conduct their audits and assessments to ensure organizations are adhering to regulations.

Organizations must be prepared for these external audits and provide the necessary documentation and evidence of compliance.

Maintaining accurate records and documentation is a critical aspect of navigating regulatory frameworks.

Organizations should keep records of all compliance-related activities, including policies, training, audits, and incident reports.

This documentation serves as proof of compliance and can be crucial in the event of an audit or investigation.

Effective communication is another key element of regulatory compliance.

Organizations should establish clear lines of communication with regulatory authorities and be prepared to report any non-compliance issues promptly.

Transparency and cooperation can help mitigate potential penalties and legal actions.

Regular training and education for employees are essential to ensure that everyone within the organization understands the importance of compliance and their role in maintaining it.

Training programs should cover relevant regulations, policies, and procedures, and should be updated regularly to reflect changes in the regulatory landscape.

Organizations must also monitor regulatory developments closely.

Laws and regulations are subject to change, and staying informed about these changes is critical for ongoing compliance.

Many organizations subscribe to regulatory intelligence services or engage legal counsel to provide updates and guidance on regulatory changes.

Another aspect of navigating regulatory frameworks is risk management.

Organizations must assess the risks associated with non-compliance and take steps to mitigate those risks.

This may involve conducting risk assessments, implementing additional controls, or purchasing insurance to cover potential liabilities.

Ethical behavior and corporate responsibility are essential considerations when navigating regulatory frameworks.

Organizations should not view compliance as a mere checkbox exercise but as a commitment to ethical conduct and responsible business practices.

Compliance efforts should align with an organization's values and principles.

In some cases, organizations may go beyond the minimum requirements of regulations to demonstrate their dedication to social and environmental responsibility.

External certifications and audits from independent third parties can also enhance an organization's reputation and trustworthiness in the eyes of customers, partners, and investors.

In summary, navigating regulatory frameworks and compliance standards is a multifaceted challenge that requires a proactive and holistic approach.

Organizations must understand the specific regulations that apply to their industry and geography, establish a compliance management framework, maintain accurate records, communicate effectively, provide ongoing training, monitor regulatory developments, manage risks, and uphold ethical behavior.

By embracing these principles, organizations can not only meet their regulatory obligations but also build a reputation for ethical conduct and responsible business practices.

Achieving and maintaining compliance in auditing is a critical objective for organizations of all sizes and across various industries.

Compliance refers to the adherence to laws, regulations, industry standards, and internal policies that govern an organization's operations.

The audit process plays a pivotal role in ensuring that an organization is compliant with these requirements.

Auditors are responsible for evaluating an organization's financial statements, internal controls, and adherence to relevant laws and regulations.

To achieve compliance in auditing, organizations must follow several key principles and best practices.

First and foremost, it's essential to establish a robust internal control system.

Internal controls are the policies and procedures put in place to safeguard assets, ensure the accuracy of financial reporting, and prevent fraud and errors.

These controls are a fundamental component of compliance, as they help an organization meet its regulatory obligations and mitigate risks.

An organization should document its internal controls comprehensively and regularly assess their effectiveness.

Documentation provides transparency and accountability, enabling auditors to evaluate the controls' design and operating effectiveness.

Moreover, organizations must have a clear understanding of the specific regulations that apply to their industry and jurisdiction.

Laws and regulations can vary significantly from one country to another and even within different regions of the same country.

Being aware of the applicable laws and regulations is the first step toward compliance.

Once an organization identifies the relevant regulations, it should integrate them into its policies and procedures.

This alignment ensures that the organization's operations are consistently in line with legal requirements.

In addition to legal compliance, organizations often need to adhere to industry-specific standards and best practices.

For example, healthcare organizations must comply with the Health Insurance Portability and Accountability Act (HIPAA), while financial institutions must follow the guidelines set forth by regulatory bodies like the Financial Industry Regulatory Authority (FINRA).

To stay current with evolving regulations and industry standards, organizations should allocate resources to regulatory compliance management.

This may involve hiring compliance officers or teams responsible for monitoring, interpreting, and implementing changes in regulations and standards.

Compliance officers play a crucial role in ensuring that an organization is always aware of its obligations and adapts to regulatory changes.

Regular training and education programs for employees are essential to achieving and maintaining compliance.

Employees should be educated about the organization's policies, procedures, and ethical standards.

Training programs help employees understand their responsibilities and the potential consequences of non-compliance.

Furthermore, organizations should establish a clear reporting mechanism for employees to raise compliance concerns or report violations.

Whistleblower policies protect employees who report wrongdoing and encourage a culture of accountability.

Auditing is an integral part of the compliance process.

Regular audits help organizations assess their level of compliance, identify areas of improvement, and mitigate potential risks.

External auditors, such as those from accounting firms, can provide an independent evaluation of an organization's financial statements and internal controls.

These audits offer assurance to stakeholders, including shareholders, investors, and regulators, that the organization is operating in compliance with established standards.

However, organizations can also conduct internal audits as a proactive measure.

Internal audits focus on assessing the effectiveness of internal controls and ensuring that policies and procedures are followed.

Auditors can recommend improvements and help organizations correct deficiencies.

Additionally, organizations should maintain comprehensive records of their compliance efforts, including audit reports, documentation of internal controls, and evidence of training and education programs.

Accurate record-keeping is crucial in demonstrating compliance to external parties, such as regulatory authorities and potential investors.

Periodic risk assessments are another essential component of compliance in auditing.

Organizations should evaluate the risks associated with non-compliance, both from a financial and reputational perspective.

Risk assessments can help organizations prioritize their compliance efforts and allocate resources effectively.

It's also advisable to perform mock audits or readiness assessments to ensure that the organization is prepared for external audits or regulatory inspections.

These practice audits can uncover weaknesses that need to be addressed before a real audit occurs.

To maintain compliance in auditing, organizations should be vigilant about staying up-to-date with changes in regulations, laws, and industry standards.

This requires ongoing monitoring and proactive adjustments to policies and procedures.

Regular communication with regulatory bodies and industry associations can provide valuable insights into upcoming changes and expectations.

Furthermore, organizations should establish a culture of compliance that encourages ethical behavior and a commitment to following established rules and regulations.

Senior leadership should set an example by prioritizing compliance and fostering a culture of accountability.

Employees at all levels should understand that compliance is not optional but a fundamental part of their roles.

In summary, achieving and maintaining compliance in auditing is a multifaceted endeavor that involves various stakeholders, including employees, management, auditors, and regulatory bodies.

It requires a proactive approach, strong internal controls, ongoing training and education, effective communication, and a commitment to ethical behavior.

Compliance is not a one-time event but an ongoing process that evolves with changing regulations and industry standards.

By following best practices and principles, organizations can ensure that they operate within the boundaries of the law and maintain the trust and confidence of their stakeholders.

Chapter 10: Real-World Insights and Ethical Hacking Success Stories

Examining notable ethical hacking cases provides valuable insights into the real-world applications and implications of ethical hacking practices. These cases shed light on the importance of ethical hacking in identifying vulnerabilities, securing critical systems, and preventing cyber threats.

One of the most famous ethical hacking cases is the "Stuxnet" attack, discovered in 2010. Stuxnet was a sophisticated computer worm designed to target Iran's nuclear facilities. It is widely believed to have been developed by a nation-state, possibly the United States and Israel, to disrupt Iran's nuclear program. Ethical hackers played a crucial role in analyzing Stuxnet, understanding its capabilities, and developing countermeasures to mitigate its impact.

Another notable case is the "Heartbleed" vulnerability, which was discovered in 2014. Heartbleed affected the OpenSSL encryption software widely used to secure internet communication. Ethical hackers identified and reported the vulnerability, leading to prompt fixes and patches to protect sensitive data from potential exploitation.

In 2015, the "Ashley Madison" data breach made headlines worldwide. Hackers gained unauthorized access to the Ashley Madison website, a platform for individuals seeking extramarital affairs, and exposed sensitive user information. This incident highlighted the importance of ethical hacking in identifying vulnerabilities before malicious actors can exploit them.

The "Equifax" data breach of 2017 was another significant case. Hackers exploited a vulnerability in Equifax's website, exposing the personal and financial data of millions of individuals. Ethical hackers played a crucial role in uncovering the vulnerability and helping Equifax address the issue to protect affected individuals.

In 2018, the "Facebook-Cambridge Analytica" scandal raised concerns about data privacy and user consent. Ethical hacking practices, combined with investigative journalism, revealed how personal data from millions of Facebook users had been harvested without their knowledge or consent. This case led to increased awareness of data privacy and the need for ethical hacking to protect user information.

The "WannaCry" ransomware attack of 2017 was a global cybersecurity crisis. Ethical hackers played a vital role in analyzing the ransomware's code, identifying its weaknesses, and developing decryption tools to help affected organizations recover their data without paying a ransom. This incident showcased the collaborative efforts of ethical hackers and cybersecurity professionals in responding to large-scale cyber threats.

Ethical hackers have also been involved in uncovering vulnerabilities in popular software and devices. For example, the "Meltdown" and "Spectre" vulnerabilities, discovered in 2018, affected a wide range of processors used in computers and mobile devices. Ethical hackers contributed to the responsible disclosure of these vulnerabilities and worked with technology companies to release patches and updates.

The "NotPetya" ransomware attack of 2017 had widespread implications, affecting businesses and organizations globally. Ethical hackers played a role in investigating the attack's origins and providing insights into its techniques. This case demonstrated the need for organizations to bolster their cybersecurity defenses and collaborate with ethical hackers to proactively address vulnerabilities.

Ethical hacking has also been instrumental in uncovering vulnerabilities in internet-of-things (IoT) devices. As more devices become connected to the internet, ethical hackers have identified security flaws in smart home devices, medical equipment, and industrial control systems. These discoveries emphasize the importance of securing IoT devices to protect users' privacy and safety.

The "SolarWinds" cyberattack, discovered in 2020, targeted multiple U.S. government agencies and private sector organizations. Ethical hackers were involved in investigating the attack's scope, identifying the tactics used by the threat actors, and helping affected organizations recover and strengthen their cybersecurity posture.

In summary, examining notable ethical hacking cases reveals the critical role ethical hackers play in identifying vulnerabilities, mitigating cyber threats, and safeguarding sensitive data. These cases highlight the ongoing battle between ethical hackers and malicious actors in the ever-evolving landscape of cybersecurity. Ethical hacking is a vital tool in protecting individuals, organizations, and governments from cyberattacks and data breaches.

Lessons learned from ethical hacking successes provide valuable insights into the effectiveness and impact of ethical hacking practices in various contexts. These lessons shed light on the evolving nature of cybersecurity and highlight the essential principles and strategies that ethical hackers employ to safeguard digital assets and data.

One fundamental lesson from ethical hacking successes is the critical role of proactive cybersecurity measures. Ethical hackers often engage in vulnerability assessment and penetration testing to identify and address security weaknesses before malicious actors can exploit them. This proactive approach enables organizations to fortify their defenses and reduce the risk of data breaches and cyberattacks.

Another important lesson is the significance of collaboration between ethical hackers and organizations. Ethical hackers work closely with businesses, government agencies, and other entities to understand their specific security needs and tailor their efforts accordingly. This partnership allows ethical hackers to provide targeted solutions and recommendations to enhance cybersecurity.

Ethical hacking successes also underscore the value of continuous learning and skill development in the cybersecurity field. Ethical hackers continually update their knowledge and expertise to stay ahead of emerging threats and vulnerabilities. This commitment to learning ensures that ethical hackers remain effective in their roles and can adapt to evolving cyber risks.

Additionally, ethical hacking successes highlight the importance of ethical guidelines and principles. Ethical hackers adhere to a strict code of ethics that prioritizes legality, transparency, and respect for privacy. These principles guide their actions and ensure that their efforts align with ethical standards while helping organizations secure their digital assets.

The use of cutting-edge tools and technologies is another lesson learned from ethical hacking successes. Ethical hackers leverage advanced cybersecurity tools to conduct thorough assessments, identify vulnerabilities, and simulate cyberattacks. These tools enable ethical hackers to provide comprehensive insights and recommendations to enhance security measures.

Ethical hacking successes also emphasize the need for clear communication between ethical hackers and stakeholders. Ethical hackers must effectively convey their findings, risks, and recommendations to organizations in a comprehensible manner. This communication ensures that organizations can take informed actions to address security vulnerabilities.

Furthermore, ethical hacking successes showcase the importance of incident response preparedness. Even with proactive security measures in place, organizations may still face cyber threats. Ethical hackers assist organizations in developing incident response plans and procedures, enabling them to react swiftly and effectively to security incidents.

The integration of ethical hacking into a comprehensive cybersecurity strategy is a valuable lesson learned from successful engagements. Ethical hackers are not standalone entities but rather integral parts of broader cybersecurity efforts. They work in tandem with security teams, IT personnel, and management to create a unified approach to cybersecurity.

One key takeaway from ethical hacking successes is the significance of transparency and disclosure. Ethical hackers follow responsible disclosure practices, which involve reporting identified vulnerabilities to organizations or software developers rather than exploiting them for personal gain. This responsible approach ensures that vulnerabilities can be patched promptly to protect users.

Ethical hacking successes also highlight the importance of adherence to industry standards and compliance requirements. Ethical hackers assist organizations in aligning their cybersecurity practices with relevant standards and regulations, reducing the risk of legal and regulatory penalties.

The ability of ethical hackers to adapt to evolving cyber threats is a critical lesson. Cyber threats constantly evolve, and ethical hackers must stay up-to-date with the latest attack techniques and vulnerabilities. Their ability to anticipate and counter new threats is a testament to their expertise.

Moreover, ethical hacking successes demonstrate the value of risk assessment and prioritization. Ethical hackers help organizations identify and prioritize security risks based on their potential impact and likelihood of occurrence. This risk-based approach allows organizations to allocate resources effectively to mitigate the most critical threats.

Ethical hacking successes also underscore the importance of user education and awareness. Many cybersecurity breaches result from human error or social engineering attacks. Ethical hackers often conduct security awareness training to educate users about common threats and best practices for staying secure online.

In summary, the lessons learned from ethical hacking successes provide valuable insights into the essential principles, strategies, and practices that contribute to effective cybersecurity. These lessons emphasize the proactive nature of ethical hacking, the importance of collaboration, adherence to ethical guidelines, and the continuous pursuit of knowledge and expertise. Ethical hacking has become an indispensable tool in safeguarding digital assets and data in an ever-evolving threat landscape.

Conclusion

In "Cyber Auditing Unleashed: Advanced Security Strategies for Ethical Hackers," we embarked on a journey through the realm of cybersecurity, delving deep into the intricacies of ethical hacking and advanced security auditing. Across the four books that comprise this comprehensive bundle, we explored the cutting-edge tactics, techniques, and insights that empower ethical hackers to protect digital ecosystems and combat cyber threats effectively.

In "Book 1 - Mastering Security Auditing: Advanced Tactics for Ethical Hackers," we laid the foundation for a robust understanding of the ethical hacker's role and the critical importance of advanced vulnerability assessment and penetration testing. We uncovered the complexities of network security analysis, web application auditing, and wireless network security, providing a solid grounding in the fundamentals of cybersecurity.

"Book 2 - Beyond the Basics: Advanced Security Auditing for Ethical Hackers" took us further into the depths of cybersecurity, unraveling the intricacies of cloud security auditing, insider threat detection, and post-audit reporting and remediation. We honed our expertise in these advanced areas, equipping ourselves with the knowledge and skills needed to navigate the evolving cyber landscape.

"Book 3 - Ethical Hacking Unleashed: Advanced Security Auditing Techniques" expanded our horizons by exploring web application scanning tools, SQL injection, cross-site scripting (XSS) testing, and wireless network enumeration. We uncovered the secrets of mitigating wireless vulnerabilities and delved into the nuances of cloud service models, providing a holistic understanding of advanced security auditing.

Finally, in "Book 4 - Security Auditing Mastery: Advanced Insights for Ethical Hackers," we reached the pinnacle of our journey, where we explored insider threat indicators, behavioral analytics, and user monitoring. We gained expertise in documentation, reporting, and effective remediation strategies, essential for safeguarding digital environments.

As we conclude this bundle, it's essential to recognize that the world of cybersecurity is ever-evolving. The threats we face are dynamic, and so too must be our defenses. The knowledge and skills acquired throughout these books empower ethical hackers to adapt and stay ahead of emerging threats. By embracing ethical hacking principles and adhering to a strong code of ethics, we contribute to a safer digital world.

Remember, the pursuit of cybersecurity excellence is not just a profession; it's a commitment to protecting individuals, organizations, and society as a whole from the perils of the digital age. "Cyber Auditing Unleashed" equips you with the tools to be a guardian of the digital realm, a sentinel of security, and a steward of ethical hacking principles.

As you embark on your own journey in the world of ethical hacking and security auditing, may the knowledge gained from these books serve as a beacon of guidance and inspiration. With unwavering dedication and continuous learning, you can make a profound impact in the ever-evolving field of cybersecurity. The path ahead is challenging, but it is also rewarding, for you have the power to protect, defend, and secure the digital world for generations to come.

www.ingramcontent.com/pod-product-compliance
Lightning Source LLC
Chambersburg PA
CBHW071234050326
40690CB00011B/2111